Minding Your Spiritual Business

Minding Your Spiritual Business

Life Stories With Life Sense

Steven J. Wunderink

Writers Club Press
New York Lincoln Shanghai

Minding Your Spiritual Business
Life Stories With Life Sense

Writers Club Press
an imprint of iUniverse, Inc.

For information address:
iUniverse, Inc.
2021 Pine Lake Road, Suite 100
Lincoln, NE 68512
www.iuniverse.com

ISBN: 0-595-26336-4

Printed in the United States of America

Cover art by Kenton McDonald. (2002)

Ken McDonald has been an artist all of his life and has owned art galleries in Las Vegas since 1985. As a child he was inspired by his older brother who was a renowned, published cartoonist. As an impressionist, he paints in oils, acrylics, and watercolors. His paintings can be found in galleries and private collections nationwide. He is a teacher and art historian, has jurored numerous art shows, and has always had an affection for the art of caricature. He is presently the art director of the new Widmen Galleries in Las Vegas, where he also conducts regular art classes. For further information on his teaching schedule, you can reach him at Widmen Galleries, 702-795-0003.

To Mom and Dad
    My head was thick
    I didn't learn quick
    But you kept with me
    So that I would see
    The sense behind the schtick

CONTENTS

PREFACE

Spiritual Business is…

those thoughts and ideas that transcend the walls of churches, businesses, and even your home. Spiritual Business is the thing in your life where you go, "Yea, I knew that!" and then you slap yourself on the forehead.

Spiritual Business covers those ideas that somehow get put up on a shelf in the back room closet of our minds and emerge too often AFTER we should have thought of them.

Spiritual Business is for those who want to succeed in business—and in life.

Steven J. Wunderink

CHAPTER ONE

Building Your House Upon a Rock

I grew up on a farm in Indiana with five brothers and two sisters. One of my play areas was the corncrib. The corncrib was a large room made of a cement floor and slatted wood sides. Farmers would put ears of corn in the crib to dry and wait until they had the need of the corn, either for grinding into food for animals or shelling into grain for the market. The biggest problem with the corncrib was that the cement floor was cracked and that left an open invitation to the entire farm rats to come and chow down. The crib would often be infested with rats; I can even remember one crawling up my pant leg. The pressure of the corn in the crib was too much; it cracked the foundation and let in all the rats.

Later, as modern farm technology took over, my father decided to build grain bins. These are large, round, metal buildings also on a cement foundation. I can remember asking my father why he built the bins where he did and his answer was that it was the best ground. It was hard clay that would support the foundation of cement so it would not crack the way the crib did. The bins with a firm foundation held tons of grain while the cribs with the shallow foundation cracked to let the rats in.

In the Bible Jesus tells the story of the "wise" man who built his house upon a rock and the "foolish" man who built his house upon the sand. When the wind and the rain came, the sandy house went down and the rocky one stood fast.

Think back on the <u>Three Little Pigs</u> fairy tale. Which house handled the big, bad wolf?

What is the foundation of your life? When the pressure is on, the winds and rain come, and the big, bad wolf is knocking and the rats are hungry, what is it that you fall back on? What is left to build on when the world crumbles?

The Mind of a Millionaire

I like to pass along info that I glean from books. Sometimes I might even give credit to the writers...

I am reading a book entitled *The Millionaire Mind* by Tom Stanley. I enjoyed his previous book, *The Millionaire Next Door*, which dealt with how you probably don't realize that some of the people who live in your neighborhood are millionaires. His thesis is they live like they only make fifty grand a year, but their bottom line is actually over a million a year. The new book includes interviews of some of these people to see what makes them tick, and what it is that allowed them to achieve such high levels of income. Most people would list the following:

1. A great job
2. A high IQ
3. Inherited it
4. Luck
5. Investing

But these are not the criteria noted on the lists of the millionaires. In fact, many of their answers tend to be the opposite. It is not the "A" students who are the majority of millionaires; it is the "C" students. It is not luck, the lottery, or a great job. Most of the millionaires never found the right job, and bounced from one to another. Very few inherited their wealth; less than 15 percent.

So what is on the list? How did they become millionaires? Well, I think the list may surprise you, but then again, maybe not. The list will make sense if you think about it. It is a great list to tell you how to become a millionaire, but also a great list to tell you how to live your life. Here goes:

1. Integrity—being honest with all people
2. Discipline—applying self-control
3. Social skills—getting along with ALL people
4. A supportive spouse—kind of self-explanatory
5. Hard work—more than the average hard worker

So follow these five steps and make a million dollars, or follow these five steps and you will realize a million bucks isn't that important after all.

I Remember Grandpa

Many of the fondest memories of my childhood years involved my grandpa. Grandpa was tall and thin, and had a laugh that would make you laugh even if you didn't hear or understand the joke. His eyes stayed bright even when the skin of his face drew tight around his bones. If you saw him, you would make fun of his hairstyle. Towards the end of his life the part in his hair got closer and closer to his ear; eventually just a fraction above it. When the wind blew, the part that barely covered his balding head flew over to his opposite shoulder. Do you get the picture of Grandpa?

Grandpa taught me to shoot pool. He had a pool table in his basement, and while he could still manage the stairs he would join my high school friends and me around the table for a game of cutthroat or pairs pool. He hit the ball hard and straight, all the while complaining, "That's an awful lot of green between me and that ball." I used to skip some church school classes with my friends and shoot pool at Grandpa's house. I don't know if he knew, but he never turned us away. After some milk and cookies upstairs with Grandma, we would head to the basement for pool. When he met my wife the first time, he told her, "Never take life too seriously, because you never get out of it alive anyway." Grandpa proved that true when he died in his bed at the age of 96. I couldn't make it to his funeral so I sent flowers with this note:

> While flowers are a poor replacement
> For my presence and my love
> This life's a poor substitute
> For the joy and peace above
>
> Grandpa's body is now alive
> With no tears or pain
> I'll see Jesus first and then
> I'll find Grandpa's smile again

Hope. Hope is the strongest foundation you can rest on. What do you hope in?

Mixing Kids and Concrete

We poured concrete for a patio this week. We spent a lot of time wheel barrowing the cement to the place, dumping it, shaking it down and, finally, finishing it. But before we could do that I had to put in a lot of hard work in preparation. Before the concrete came I had to dig out the clay that was where the concrete was going. Then I had to set up forms and level the area out. Then my wife Frankie wanted some water on the patio for some planted pots, so I had to run some pipes under the forms. Finally we were ready to pour.

This reminded me of my kids and many other things in life. If you want the best cement patio possible, you need to put in the work and pre-work necessary. If you want your child to have the best possible you have to put in the work and the pre-work. It doesn't just happen. You have to lay the groundwork. You have to set the boundaries in the same way you set your forms. If the cement goes beyond the forms, it's rough, unfinished. It's often thrown away because it's not useful for anything. Now that would be a rather harsh thing to do to a kid, but think about it. If your kids have NO boundaries...

One of my kids was a climber; we could not keep the kid in his crib. He just kept climbing out and hurting himself. He went beyond his boundaries and got hurt (sometimes because of spankings from Mom and Dad). I remember, growing up, my dad said, "Absolutely no swimming on Sunday." We kept trying to play with that boundary, sitting on the edge with our feet in the pool and walking around it, getting a suntan. Inevitably, one of us would "fall" in, pulling the other one in, or whatever. The pain came later when we couldn't swim for a whole week afterwards.

Another way to stretch the analogy is in the setup time. Cement has a very limited time before it sets up, hardens, and makes it nearly impossible to change. With kids you have limited time as well. While the kids are young and preteens, they can still be molded and shaped. The younger they are the better chance you have to shape character. An old proverb says this: "Train up a child in the way he should go, and when he is old, he will not depart from it." To get the idea of just how fast you lose your ability to influence kids, come over to my house—I'll show you how hard cement gets—and how soon. Well, maybe not...just spend the time with YOUR kids.

Good Ruts

I have a definition of integrity for you. But first...let me tell you story.

Growing up on a farm in Indiana I had plenty of exposure to driving. I starting driving a tractor through the hayfield at about 8 or 9 years old. I remember that my dad would have to hop onto the tractor to turn it around for me and get it going down the field straight again. His instructions to me were brief: "Don't run over the hay bales." I could only steer. To stop I had to climb off the seat, and while standing, pull back the hand clutch.

Indiana gets a lot of rain. The dirt roads to the fields would turn to mud and getting equipment out to the fields became a challenge. You would have to know when to speed up, when to let the wheels spin, and when to slow down and let them regain traction again. Otherwise you would be stuck and there is nothing worse than getting stuck on the road to the field. No cell phones not even CBs to communicate—you had to walk, one way or the other. I became an expert at finding the best place to drive through the muddy spots. I found them to be in what you'd think would be the worst place. When the dirt road was dry, ruts would be created simply because they were the shortest distance between two points. When it was dry you avoided those ruts because they were bumpy, tough to stay in because your wheels were different, or simply hard on the tires. But when it rained, those same places were the best for driving on, because those ruts were also the hardest packed dirt. While all around the ruts turned to a muddy mess, the ruts themselves were packed so hard that the water ran right off them. So the best place to stay when the rains came was on the ruts—the packed hard places— and you would not get stuck.

Ruts have a bad connotation in our society. When you are in a rut, you are in a bad place. But I would suggest that integrity is simply being in a good rut. When you are in that rut it doesn't matter what winds and rains may come, it doesn't matter that others are getting stuck around you, what matters is staying the course—not wandering, not experimenting—and getting to where you are going. Many will ask you to compromise your integrity, to get out of that rut you are in, and experiment. "Try something new!" A person with integrity will answer, "No, that's fine, I'm happy right here, stuck in my rut." My rut of honesty, my rut of fidelity, my rut of tenderness, my rut of care and concern.

What kind of rut are you in? Is it time to start a new, good one now, BEFORE the winds and rains come?

Feeling Badly

I was sick this week…I mean SICK! It was so bad on Tuesday that my chest still hurt on Saturday from the pulled muscles. The muscles were pulled by involuntarily constricting at an uncontrollable rate to the point of expelling everything that was contained in my stomach. (Was that a polite way to say "throw-up" or what?)

I lay in bed or on my La-Z-boy with varying degrees of feelings. At first I felt wrong. Then I felt a little funny. Then came the feeling I might be sick. Then came the KNOWING I was sick. Then came the wishing I wasn't sick anymore. Then came the pleading for not being sick anymore. Then I felt like I was going to die. Then I KNEW I was going to die. Then I thought dead would be a good thing. Then after what seemed like a new millennium, I realized I wasn't feeling as bad anymore, until finally food and water were no longer my enemy. I am sure all of you can relate to these feelings. Now I am feeling fine (outside of the remnant sore muscles), and looking back on that Tuesday as a humorous memory. My death wish is gone, and the pounds of weight I lost are being gleefully put back on again.

So how can I put a spiritual message to this story, you may be asking? Well, here goes…

I think I want to use this story to talk to you about faith. You see, faith is the "knowledge of things unseen." Faith is being "certain of things hoped for." Do you see anything about "feelings" in the definition of faith? In fact, I would dare say that faith is the OPPOSITE of feelings.

Your faith in your God, your faith in other people, and your faith in yourself have nothing to do with feelings. Your faith is a "sure" or "certain" knowledge. If faith was tied to feelings, then my experiences this week showed that when I felt well my faith in God was good; but when I felt badly, my faith was bad; when I wanted to die, my faith in God was gone.

You cannot depend on your feelings, good or bad. You cannot rest your faith and your beliefs on feelings, because feelings change with the wind (and the flu bug). If I want to have a strong and pleasant feeling, I stick my hands in hot water or eat a bite of a fresh blueberry tart. Your feelings can and often do fool you, and sometimes they even make you sick to your stomach.

A Teacher's Brain

A teacher was attempting to prove to her third graders that God doesn't exist. "Johnny" she asked, "can you see the chalkboard?"

"Yes," said Johnny.

"Can you see that tree outside?"

"Yes."

"Can you see or feel God?"

"Well, no."

"There, you see! God doesn't exist because you cannot see or feel him!" the teacher said triumphantly.

"But teacher," said Johnny. "I can't see or touch your brain either, does that mean it doesn't exist too?"

I have digital phone. The salesman told me that these phones send a digital signal up to a satellite, it bounces off that back to their receiving station, and then through the regular phone lines to reach the party I am dialing. All of this happens in a few seconds.

I have a friend in Africa that I email. I can type an email and press send, and he will get the email in Africa faster than I can run to the fridge in my house for a soda.

The golf course I often golf on is close to an airport. I see a metal tube weighing hundreds of tons actually floating over my head as I tee off.

Is it really so hard to believe that God exists? Is it really so hard to believe that something we can't touch or see is real?

I have come to believe that THE most important question that you have to ask yourself is: Does God exist? I mean REALLY exist? If you really believe that God exists, I mean really believe that, how would that change your actions? Or would it? I find that most of the people I run into are like my kids when they were young. They would cover their own eyes and yell, "You can't see me, you can't see me!" There is evidence of God everywhere. Are you covering your eyes?

Hanging Your Hope

Hope.

Hope is a name. I've known a few girls with the name of Hope.

Hope is a college in Michigan.

Hope is a fragrance—a perfume with a particular scent.

What is hope? You hope something happens or doesn't happen. You say, "I hope so" so often you can't keep track of it.

Let's try to wrap our minds around hope. Hope is your desire for a preferred outcome. You want something to happen in the future. You don't know if it will or not, but you sure would like it to. You "hope" it happens. Hope is a verb, an action that you take. I hope you read this. I hope my kids grow to be strong and confident adults. I hope my wife and I can grow very old together. I hope, you hope, we hope...

But hope is more than just a verb, it is also a noun. I have hope. Do you? This kind of hope is based on something you have confidence in—something bigger, stronger, or more intelligent than you. This narrows hope, as a noun, to something reliable, capable of handling your hopes.

People try to hang hope on money and find it is a pretty weak hook. Others try to hang hope on a job or on the NEXT job or the next move or the next promotion, but those are weak hooks to hang hope on. So what is strong enough to hang our hopes on?

How about family, love, and God? Go to a funeral and you will see the hooks hope is hung on. It is right out there in the open. Family surrounds you, love fills you, and God takes care of eternity.

So what do you hang your hope on?

Don't Complicate It!

Fred Rogers of *Mr. Roger's Neighborhood* once said, "Life is deep and simple, what the world gives you is shallow and complicated."

I like that quote. I like it because that is what we humans have a tendency to do. We take the simple things of life and pour on complication like my kids pour syrup on pancakes. What we end up with is a sticky mess. I like the quote because we humans make shallow what should be deep. While it may look the same on the surface, whey you dive in you find out how shallow it is.

There is a story about a truck driver who tried to get his semi under a bridge that was too low. It got stuck and wedged tight. The police called the fire department, the fire department called a construction crew with cranes, and they all stood around trying to figure out how to lift the bridge or take apart the truck. They held up traffic for hours before a little child leaned out of the window of his parents' minivan and said, "Why don't you just let the air out of the tires?"

Psychiatrists tell you that it was your parents, a trauma growing up, your genes, or your environment that caused you to have all these psychological problems. I think all you really need is a good friend to share with, to tell you the truth when you need to hear it, and to love you no matter what—simple.

It is the same with spiritual matters. The concepts of faith and belief have been much debated and abused. Many religions pour on the complications and make them shallow by arguing about what to wear, who may come, and how you need to speak. Here is one of the deepest, yet simplest, truths I have ever heard.

> Jesus loves me this I know
> For the Bible tells me so
> Little ones to him belong
> They are weak but he is strong
> Yes, Jesus loves me
> Yes, Jesus loves me
> Yes, Jesus loves me
> The Bible tells me so

Simple, deep truth. Don't complicate it.

September 11, 2001

We will all remember this date for the rest of our lives, what we were doing and where we were when the towers came down.

I am encouraged. And let me tell you why.

I do a lot of speaking about making sure that your foundation is stable, about making sure that you build your life on a firm foundation so that when the winds and waves come, when the pressure is piled on, when the big bad wolf comes along to huff and puff; you have a firm foundation left after it all.

What's left in our country since 9/11 is our foundation. Contrary to what the terrorists were going for, I saw our foundations exposed for one of the only times in my life. We Americans have been fighting and bickering about everything from who won the presidential election to whether you like Coke or Pepsi. We have fought among ourselves like children.

So what came out of the rubble?

After the smoke cleared, standing in the rubble, I saw America's foundation, long hidden in our squabbles. I saw the courage of firemen and police running TO disaster and not away from it. I saw "service" in the long lines of those all over the country: lines to donate blood, to give help, to heal, to give money. I saw love in the tears of friends and family, even in strangers. I saw patriotism in flags everywhere but on the shelves in stores. But most of all, I saw God at the foundation of the United States. Picture this: casino marquees in Las Vegas, for the first time ever, flashing the word "GOD" repeatedly. "In God We Trust." "God bless America." "One Nation Under God."

I am encouraged because I've seen the structure that made the United States come down and what was left—walking out of the dust and rubble—was beautiful. Now, let's rebuild on that foundation and we will continue to be a great country.

Banging the Head

I was traveling recently, and since September 11, 2001 that has taken on a whole new meaning. There was increased security at all three airports I was in. My briefcase was checked for bomb residue both coming and going. I had a suspicious-looking object on the way back and they made me open it. It turned out to be a roll of the new statehood quarters I had picked up.

As I flew, I noticed a lot of nervous people. The plane was mostly full, and everybody was nervous until the people got into the terminal. It was kind of weird. I remember looking ahead from my aisle row seat into the first class area and at the cockpit door, wondering what I would do if a guy with a knife was there. I imagine that a lot of the passengers did the same.

Then I noticed something that made me smile. In front of me walking up into the ramp of the airplane was a mom with two kids. One of the kids was walking with a cool, colored, pull cart carry-on. He was probably five or six. The mom pushed a stroller with a baby, no more than one. I helped her as she struggled getting her baby out of the stroller so they could stow it, while watching the boy and her own carry-ons. She seemed to juggle five things at once and she was getting quite harried. Purse and carry-on hooked on her shoulder, the young boy's hand in hers, and the baby in her other arm, and she proceeded into the small door of the airplane. I offered to help, but she said she was okay. So far not too funny, right? But I haven't told you about the baby yet. See, the baby was fast asleep; I mean FAST asleep, snoring and everything. The baby survived the transition from the stroller to his mother's arms; quite a rough transition with all she was doing. He was awkwardly laying in his mother's tight clutch, and I could see the child's face as I followed behind. His head and his arm came out from his mother's embrace. As she entered the plane, because his head and arm were sticking out and she had other things on her mind, she banged his head and arm on the doorway going into the plane so hard all could hear it. She stopped to take care of the inevitable wail from the child but there was not a sound. He didn't even wake up! She looked at me, I smiled, so did she, and the whole group disappeared into the plane.

Now THAT is a peaceful, deep, secure sleep. It didn't matter to the baby what was going on all around him or even to him. He slept, peaceful and easy. Now tell me, what happens to the peace and security that we are born with and grow up with? While all the adults were nervous, the baby was asleep like a…well, like a baby. Hmm. Whose arms are you secure in during these times?

Commencement Address

Dear Graduates,

In an effort to provide you with a nitro boost of momentum as you enter the rat race, let me offer you a few words of encouragement and advice. Some of these are my own, some are variations on statements of others, and most are just plain stolen:

- If you do stop to smell the roses watch out for the bees.
- As you walk through life, focus on your own clumsiness first then worry about those trying to trip you.
- Never let school interfere with education.
- Never let education stop.
- Consider yourself in a constant state of indebtedness.
- Take chances.
- Shampoo even though your hair stays in place better when you don't.
- Take care of your teeth.
- If you wear glasses or contacts, get laser surgery. It is the best thing since sliced bread and gives you a whole new look at the world.
- Earn it, don't expect it.
- Don't grow up too fast, it's hard on the clothes.
- Take responsibility, take ownership, and the world will be yours.

- Fail creatively and regularly.
- Keep track of smells.
- Compliment women and let men win.
- Your perfect mate exists only in your mind. Adjust your thinking, then BECOME the perfect mate and choices will flock to you.
- Drive with the windows down sometimes.
- Read.
- Take control of addictions in private or they WILL become public.
- Eat slowly.
- Don't confuse your wants with your needs.
- Hug.
- Practice random acts of kindness.
- Do the common and usual things with such consistency that they become uncommon and unusual.
- Laugh a lot, even when it isn't funny, but still take your medicine.

There you go, just a small taste of the random Post-It notes stuck to the inner walls of my head. Take the ones that resonate and throw out the ones that irritate. And above all, graduates, hang on to those funny hats. You can use them later for taping and mudding drywall, as Frisbees, and even to serve your roommates chips and dip.

We're Such Wimps

Our air conditioner doesn't work well. It got to 106° in Las Vegas this past week—in the shade! That is hot. Whether it is a dry heat or not, it is still hot. My family and I "suffered" in the heat, every now and again checking the vents to see if anything mildly resembling coolness was making it through to our stifling rooms. Fans moved the hot air around the house but failed to create any kind of comfort. I thought of my eighth-grade science teacher saying, "Evaporation is a cooling process." Well, it's a poor one.

What wimps we are! Air conditioning is only a few decades old but now you cannot buy a car without it. Even my brother's farm tractors have air conditioning! When I was a kid we had to suffer through the heat and dust just to coax up a few bushels of corn. Now my brother gets hundreds of bushels an acre sitting in an air-conditioned, computerized, stereo-filled cab. They probably have La-Z-Boy chairs in them now too. (I should find out whether my brother reads this book or not from this last comment—yikes!)

I drive in my air-conditioned truck listening to books on CD for the easy three-hour drive to Los Angeles for meetings, and comfortably drive back. There are a few times when I pause and look out the sealed, tinted windows and wonder, "How in the world did people one hundred or one hundred fifty years ago find the El Cajon pass? How did they make their way in covered wagons and hiking through the mountains that even stress my modern-day vehicle?" These pioneers did unbelievable things to settle new places in a new country, and here I am whining about how hot it is in my house.

Our parents all used the old "When I was young…," or "I had to walk to school in the snow, summer and winter, uphill both ways, wild wolves chasing me for sport, following the mammoth tracks and carefully avoiding the twenty-year-old bullies still in eighth grade." But the truth is, we ARE wimps compared to our parents' generation, and especially our grandparents' generation. Sure, we have our own problems, with school violence, rampant disease, and terrorism, but imagine losing half your brothers and sisters to childhood illnesses, losing your parents to hard labor, fourteen-hour workdays, no education, no computers, and no air conditioning. When people say they long for the "good ol' days" you know they don't know what they are talking about.

So it's time for us to toughen up and realized how good we have it. It is also time to thank our parents and grandparents for building this world we now live in and enjoy. Go and see them, give them a long hug, and say thank you. That is probably the least wimpy thing we can do.

Good Tired

I must have put over two hundred miles on my truck the other day. I ran from this place to that place and back again, then did it over for the next meeting and the next conference, then back to this place and…well, you get the idea. I am tired. I am tired of sitting in my truck, tired of meetings, and all I want to do is sit in front of a newspaper with a Diet Coke and read. I just feel like I didn't get anything done, with the entire running around, I didn't get anything done.

Have you ever had those days? Days that were so filled with things to do and places to go and by the end of it you feel like you haven't done a thing? Have you had those days? I have, and they make me tired at the end of them; BAD tired.

Bad tired is when you feel exhausted for all the wrong reasons. So, obviously, GOOD tired is when you are tired for all the right reasons. I remember working on the farm, shoveling corn, all day. It seemed like the grain bin had an endless supply of corn. The augur would only reach so far to get the corn out of the bin; the rest was up to young, strapping, and farm boys. You would wear a scarf or mask from all the dust and chaff in the air and come out of the bin caked in a mixture of that chaff and sweat. Ahhhh…summertime on the farm. During our lunchtime we would eat a great, full meal my mother prepared, then take a fifteen-minute power nap on the floor so we didn't get furniture dirty. Miraculously and simultaneously we would awaken together, pick up our shovels and crawl back into the bin. At the end of the day you were tired, GOOD tired. Fall asleep quickly, before you hit the bed, with a smile on your face—GOOD tired.

But now I run around to my meetings and conferences and find that I need a nap, and a good night's sleep but something is wrong. I am BAD tired. The difference, I think, is what state your heart is in. Let me give you some examples:

- Laugh a lot, even when it sorrow and loss cause BAD tired
- love and helping others cause GOOD tired
- lying, deceit, and darkening of the heart causes BAD tired
- an honest day's hard work causes GOOD tired
- disconnected, rote, repetitive labor causes BAD tired
- engaged, lively, purposeful labor causes GOOD tired
- bad friends doing bad things causes BAD tired
- good friends doing good things causes GOOD tired

What state is your heart in right now? Are you heading for a good tired tonight or a bad tired? It's not too late to turn it around.

I Believe

Many people in religious and non-religious circles ask me to define things for them. One of the questions I get all the time is, "What does it mean to BELIEVE in something?" or "What does it mean to have FAITH in something?" This is a critical question because most religions require you to believe or have faith.

Let me give you Steve's definition of "belief" and "faith." I will use these words interchangeably, because if you look one up in the dictionary you get the other, and so on. To have faith means that you "act as if you agree with _____ regardless of the outward circumstances." Now you can fill in that blank with something you have faith in, or believe in.

For instance, I believe in God. That means that I must act as if I agree with God regardless of the outward circumstances. So how do I agree with God? The Bible tells me that the Christian God is loving and kind: I must agree. It tells me that God also demands perfection and I cannot match that perfection without his help: I must agree. It tells me that I must obey the Ten Commandments and the two main ones on love: I must agree. I must agree regardless of the circumstances around me, including the people who don't agree.

What do you believe in? What do you have faith in? What does your "god" require of you? Belief and faith are not nebulous, hard to grasp terms. They are the nitty-gritty of life. To act as if you agree is a matter of obedience and that is something that we all have a hard time with. To do it no matter what the outward circumstances are is a matter of perseverance, and that is even more difficult. The whole world may be against you but you must persevere if you really believe and have faith. Faith, belief, obedience, and perseverance are interconnected like your thumb and fingers on your hand. Without faith you cannot hang onto anything of value; all that is important to you will slip through your fingers. Without obedience and perseverance your faith has no bony structure to accomplish anything, it is just a flabby idea that sounds nice.

Faith is action, belief is work and not in the short term; it is a lifetime vocation and not a nice, flabby thought.

I believe I'm done with this chapter; therefore, I will act like it and quit typing.

CHAPTER TWO

Remembering the Sabbath Day

The Sabbath day is a churchy word. Sabbath was originally meant to designate Saturday. The Jews still celebrate it from sundown on Friday to sundown on Saturday. Other religions celebrate the Sabbath on Sunday; still others have their special day on Wednesday or Friday. Every day of the week is some religion's "special day."

I look at the Sabbath day a little differently. Let me explain.

Ronald Reagan once said, when harassed about taking a month off as President, "I can get 12 months of work done in 11 months, but I cannot get 12 months of work done in 12 months." Now this may sound weird, but it is true. We need to take time off, time away, because it makes us more productive when we are back working again. And time management people have told me that 1-in-7 is a pretty good ratio for time off.

Life is busy, spinning around us at an ever-increasing pace. We often get caught up in the spin and end up spinning out of control. We need to stop the top. Stop spinning for a while to catch our breath and our equilibrium. We need a Sabbath rest. We need to stop spinning so we can get a perspective on things again.

The story is told of a young man who went into the woods of Northern California to make his fortune. He found men chopping trees down for a lumber company and believed he could not only do it, but also do it better than they could. The foreman gave him the job and he bought his own, brand new axe. The first day he felled more trees then all those around him. The next, again, felled more trees. The third he had a harder time—even worked through breaks—but could only equal the other's production. By the sixth day he was struggling to keep up with even the worst of the other lumberjacks. He finally went to the foreman to quit. "I can't keep up," he said. The foreman looked at him and said, "You work real hard, son, I would hate to see you go. Let me ask you one question before you give up. When was the last time you paused to sharpen your axe?"

Are you spinning out of control? Is your productivity hurting? When is the last time you paused to sharpen your axe?

Looking Up

In my evermore-frustrating search to find an honest auto mechanic I had the opportunity to walk some of the seedier parts of town this week. For those of you who are not familiar with Las Vegas, there is a stretch of Las Vegas Blvd. (the Strip) that is kind of sad and old. That area is between the Stratosphere Casino and the rebuilt downtown. I walked that stretch twice while waiting for a bus to take me back home.

The sidewalk is stained with what looks like oil but is more likely alcohol and vomit mixed with a little blood. The store owners spray it with water daily but the stain remains. Littering the walk is garbage, collected in corners and against security fences by the wind; most of it is the enticing full color pamphlet of the strip clubs. Women with strategically-placed stars or hearts airbrushed to perfection with those "come check it out" looks on their faces. I pass a man in dirty clothes, a week-old beard, and few teeth as he smiles at me before sipping out of a brown paper bag. I smile back. The storefronts and windows are barred and locked, and in the corner of each is a crumpled, faded picture of the flag or some forgotten 9/11 symbol.

The stores are a curious mix that I don't think you will find anywhere else in the world. First you have a XXX club advertising their lap dances for only $5, next you have a wedding chapel advertising their packages which include a limo to the courthouse and free garter belt, next a rundown hotel advertising hourly rates up to monthly rates, next a tuxedo and wedding dress rental place with beat-up mannequins, followed by another hotel that advertises that Elvis slept there, then more of the same. At the bus kiosks are a mixture of the well dressed and barely dressed of every nationality. Taxis and limos go by with tourists on their way to the next casino or the next "pleasure palace," not even seeing the people who line the streets.

I stand behind a bus kiosk in the shade and eavesdrop on the conversation. Boyfriend and kid problems, that next job, where's that &*#$ bus! I get on the bus and I am taken south on the strip, past the façades of the billion dollar casinos and the busy airport, and finally to the outlet mall, where I get off with my mind reeling from the experience. Should I be mad, sad, or just plain glad I'm not a part of the scenes I just witnessed? What can we do? What should we do? Should we do anything?

Then I remembered as I passed the brown paper bag guy on the street, I nodded and gave him my standard greeting. "howya doin" never expecting an answer. He answered with "I'm doing great, it's a beautiful day isn't it?" as he looked up into the clear blue sky. I looked up too, up above the sidewalk, up above the storefronts, even above the high-rise condos and casinos in the background and I saw. I see…It took a homeless drunk to teach me that problems and garbage lie here on the sidewalks of life but the beauty and the peace comes from above. I need to look up more often.

Train Tracks

Behind my office is a train track, once a day or so a train goes by slowly, bringing with it memories like so many boxcars attached.

There were tracks on our farm in Indiana bordering our property. I would play there bringing along pennies in the hopes of a train flattening Abe Lincoln into a smooth copper pancake. I would dream of the places the train was off to and wishing I could hobo along.

Walking home from where our grade school bus dropped us off, we crossed a train track on the halfway point. I remember trying to run to the tracks as if in training, and the dogs that were on the other side of the tracks waiting to take a bite out of my faded blue jeans. I ran quite fast when the dogs were in pursuit.

I remember waiting at tracks in my parents' car, counting the number of cars in the train, knowing it was going to be an especially long one when there were three engines at the front. I remember my own, seemingly grown-up, teenage impatience as I sought ways to get around the guardrails or ignored the signals of the train bearing down.

I remember walking tracks with my kids, telling these stories, placing pennies on the tracks, and dreaming of places to go and see. "I will take a train to Hawaii someday!" said one. In our minds, trains even went to Hawaii.

Trains are magical vehicles, which is amazing because they cannot leave the tracks laid out for them. In our minds, trains take us to far-off lands and over oceans. Sadly, most rails are becoming rusty and overgrown, bridges are becoming unsafe, and fewer and fewer trains go by. Don't let that happen to the kid in your mind; the kid that longs to take that train to Hawaii or Egypt or even China. Keep the rails of your dreams free from rust and the bridges to your imagination strong and intact. I think you will find, amazingly enough, that those trips are not so unreachable as they seem. So together, lets hop on a railcar and go to Hawaii.

Church

How do you get to know somebody? How does a person go from a stranger to an acquaintance to a friend? How does that happen? Did you ever just stop and think about it?

We need to know this if we are to have any friends at all. As an introvert, I would just as soon not even make the effort. I would rather they come to me for a job interview. "Okay, have a seat. Now tell me, why do you want to be my friend and what can you contribute to this friendship?" and then "Thank you for applying, I will let you know in a few days."

Some friends we seem to be born with; they have always been here, like a close neighbor or brother or sister. Some friends you make at work. When you spend eight-plus hours together, you get to know each other pretty well. Sometimes you find friends with similar interests, like sports or clubs. On the other hand, you could do the same thing with others and they will NEVER become your friends. You don't even want them as acquaintances. Why is there a difference? You are in the same situation, same job, same neighborhood, but some become friends and others don't.

I think it is a heart thing. I've met a lot of people. We were all even in the same profession, facing many of the same problems, but there were only a few that I would call friends. We have a heart connection. It was almost like our hearts resonated to the same beat; and, yes, you can tell that. There's something about them that just feels right. The opposite is also true. There are people whose hearts grind on yours. That doesn't necessarily mean they are bad, just different. They will find other friends whose heart matches theirs.

I also think that hearts can change to resonate together, even if it is only temporary. A crowd can get that way sometimes at a sporting event or listening to a moving speech, or even a song. It can be an amazing time—to have many hearts together, in harmony, resonating in sync. In fact, this should happen every time you step into something called a church.

I Saw God this Morning

I saw something beautiful this morning. If I were a good painter, I would have driven a few miles for a better look, taken all the pictures I could, and painted on a canvas to capture it as best I could.

We had rain this week in Las Vegas, which is pretty rare for us, and it was cloudy for about three days. At this time of year it rains in the valleys and snows in the mountains. You can see on the mountain range where the cutoff is from snow to rain. The clouds broke as I looked west to the mountains. The sun shined through and was lighting up the snow with brilliance. There were bundles of clouds trying to work their way through the passes in the mountains. They were puffy white, with the stark blue sky above them. This was contrasted with the dark mountains and snow that defined every nook and cranny in the rock face. It was absolutely breathtaking.

I was walking out of a building, saw it for the first time, and just stopped and stared. People walked around me, and most mumbled and grumbled at my holding up the foot traffic. As people do, some stopped to look at what I was looking at, and they were filled with awe as well. Some stood for a few minutes and some glanced and went back to staring at the sidewalk as they passed. After a moment or two it was gone. The clouds covered our view again, and the snow-covered mountains dimmed in the haze of the day.

I saw God in the moment—not only the creator God, the one who made the mountains and the skies and clouds, but also the active and present God, the painter/artist who put together this dramatic show for me and a few others who paused to notice.

That is what Sabbath rest is all about—stopping and pausing for a few minutes from our constant stare at the hard concrete walk of life and gazing at an amazing work of the most gifted artist, an artist who crafts beauty in an instant of time just for us who take the time to notice.

Pause, look, smell and see. Take a Sabbath break.

Happily Plucking Leeches

Summer is here! School's out and life begins anew! Summer is a great time, especially for those who are still school age. It is a time of freedom and a time of relief from the pressures of classes and tests.

I remember summers in Indiana. I remember getting out of school and dumping all the notes and notebooks that had been my lifeline for the last nine months. I remember looking forward to the warm weather and the swimming pool in our backyard. When we were young, my brothers and I would play every game imaginable on the farm. If there was enough water in the ditches we would take out the old canoe and play that we were sneaking into adventure in the murky water. We would pretend to be shot and fall down the ditch bank and end up face down in the muck, laughing the whole time. We would come home to Mom with a Mason jar full of tadpoles and a few leeches to pour salt on; smiling the whole time. Gone were algebra, history, and geography. Every day was PE.

That is the way summer would start out, anyway. Reality caught up with us on the farm quickly as we got older. My father would not allow too much playtime before we would be back on the tractor cultivating or spraying the fields, or my mom would have us out in her one-hundred-acre (it seemed like) garden, pulling and hoeing weeds, and picking beans, peas, strawberries, and whatever else she would decide to punish us with. As we got older we would get jobs that would actually pay us. I would de-tassel corn for ninety-five cents an hour, then I would work at the local county fairgrounds, where my uncle was head of maintenance, and set up for the coming fair. Today, most teenagers have jobs for the summer, everything from McDonalds to office work, sometimes starting too young.

I would encourage you to go back to those carefree days of play every now and again. Even if not physically, do it mentally. Remember those times when the pressure was off and fun was on? Take mini-vacations. I know you have responsibilities, but don't forget to have JOY too. Get together with friends and family and go to the old swimming hole. Play, even if you have to use your kids or grandkids as an excuse.

In fact…I wonder if I can find that old Lego set of mine again.

Sunshine on My Shoulder

This was the first really great week of sunshine in Las Vegas this year! Not that the sun hasn't shone before this, but the temperature was in the 80s and the sun was shining. The evenings were cool but not cold. What a great week! But, like I normally do, I got a little too much sun, especially on the ever-expanding forehead. I was working around my pool and around the yard. I did a little golfing; and all of this in bright sunshine. It got to the point where shade was a happy relief from the sun, where the wind and shade were welcome comforts. After a few hours in the sun it became more oppressive than enjoyable; you know the feeling. I don't burn much, and I make sure I don't spend too much time in the sun, but I always seem to manage to burn my forehead (or fivehead, or sixhead as my daughter now calls it) where I had hair last year. It's a little rim of virgin skin forming a coast along my receding hairline. By the end of the summer that skin has toughened and darkened like the rest of my sixhead.

Shade. You never come to truly appreciate shade unless you have spent time in the hot sun. The shade in Las Vegas can be up to twenty degrees cooler than direct sunlight. Shade pushes away the oppression of the sun; shade shields you from its rays and keeps you from burning. Shade is a wonderful thing.

In the Bible, the Book of Psalms contains the metaphor of God being our shade. That metaphor is repeated often as King David, a warrior and a shepherd, knew what an oppressive sun was like. God keeps us from harm, God protects us, and God shields us from oppression. God even creates comfort in our lives.

Consider your life this week and ask yourself this question: Am I the sun or the shade to the people I love? Do I shield and protect them from harm and oppression, or do I intensify them? Don't get me wrong; there is a time when you must shine the light on your loved ones and challenge them to become more than they are right now. Your primary job, however, because you love them, is to create shade and a comfortable place for them to be.

It's starting to get hot again; I think I'll go spend time with my shade.

The Bionic Man

Remember the sound that the Bionic Man and Woman made in slow motion? "Shshshshshsh huhuhuhuhuhuh," as they leaped tall buildings, bent metal, and ran 100 mph. I can still see the shows on the viewing screen of my mind. I thought Lindsay Wagner was a babe! For those of you who don't remember the show, it was about a man (Lee Majors) and a woman (Lindsay) who had parts of their natural bodies removed and had "bionic" parts added in their places. "Bionic" is combining biological with electronic, I think. These new parts allowed them to do amazing things, such as comic book legends do, especially in capturing the bad guys.

One of the best things I've done in recent history is to get laser surgery on my eyes. I've had glasses since second grade, and my eyes had gotten progressively worse through the years to the point where my glasses resembled the Coke bottle bottoms of legend. My vision was 20/400 or something like that. Since the surgery, my vision is 20/18 in one eye and 20/25 in the other. One eye is "set" for distance and the other for reading. The surgery also took care of my astigmatism. I can now swim and go to bed with my eyes open and actually see who is next to me! What an amazing medical breakthrough!

I read in the latest edition of *Popular Science* that within two years we will have "bionic" eyes, and in ten years they will replace laser surgery. One type of bionic eye is for blind people, which uses computer technology to "see." Currently, this can only be in black and white, but it has had a dramatic positive impact on the blind. The second type of "bionic" eye involves a fake muscle wrapped around the eyeball so that muscle can contract and expand at one's command. It has a little power source located behind the ear, and with it one will not only be able to see better, but even zoom in to eagle vision and out to close-up vision. This is a true "bionic" eye!

Some people are scared about all these new advances and the rapid growth of technology, but I say, "Bring it on!" Why hold it up? Do you really think that we as a people have advanced beyond what God can handle? Do you think he is sitting on his throne in heaven, shaking his head and saying, "I don't believe it. I would have never thought they would have come up with that! What am I going to do now?" In our romp through technological history we cannot lose focus on making sure people come before science, but science and technology are GOD-GIVEN and GOD-BLESSED. God wants us to discover more and more about his creation and his universe because he knows it will bring us all back to the artist/scientist that put it all together. He smiles and says, "Hey, people, discover this!"

CHAPTER THREE

Running the Race

In junior high, I ran in track-and-field competitions. I was close enough to being a natural athlete that I didn't think I needed to work out too much for events. I loved the short races because I would not have to be in shape to run them. Back then they were called the 100-yard dash and the 220. One day, my coach told me that for this meet I was to run the 440 as well. "No problem," I said. "I can handle it." Well, I could handle the first 220 yards and was leading the pack, but then came the next 220, and I couldn't stop to catch my breath. I started to concentrate on the pain in my chest and legs that wouldn't move to my commands any more. Everything felt like extra weight holding me back. In the final stretch a runner passed me by, then another, then more. I think I finished ahead of a few kids, but not many. I ran the race, but I ran it incorrectly.

I've always enjoyed the adventure stories of attempts to climb Mount Everest. I've read many of the books on it. One of the things that they constantly talk about when climbing is the need to look up, to see where you are going but also to keep that aim, that goal in front of you. When the clouds covered the peak, the emotional impact was great. Depression set in, and many gave up when the peak was gone. It was as if the goal of the summit seemed impossible to reach when it could not be seen.

The Bible uses running the race as a metaphor of life. Paul says at the end of his life, while in jail and still encouraging others, "I have fought the good fight, I have finished the race, I have kept the faith." What better theme to have for your life as you look back. I would love to have that on my tombstone. More accurately, I would love to have earned the right to have that on my tombstone.

When you are Minding your Spiritual Business you must look at the direction your life is taking. You must run in such a way as to not run out of gas in the middle of the race. You must keep your eye on the goal or the prize, even when you cannot see them. How are you running your race?

For Such a Time as This

I am now over forty years old. I am trying to FEEL differently, but I just don't. I guess what I feel is anticipation and maybe a little excitement.

I have the feeling that I am just starting something. I have been feeling for a while now that this world is no longer in the hands of my father's generation but is in the hands of MY generation. That is both scary AND exciting. My parents fought World War II, and raised kids with little money and no TV. They helped build new communities, suburbs, and churches. They made America what it is today. The baton has been passed.

I have always been one who enjoys being in charge. I enjoy being the one upon whom the "buck stops," but I also have the tendency to take on more than I can really handle. So, as I look with anticipation at my next forty years on this earth, I see tremendous opportunities stretching out before me. Maybe a better way to put it is that I am excited to be a part of my generation, and to contribute something good to hand over to the next generation. There is nothing better than to work for good.

There is a story in Jewish and Christian scripture of a queen named Esther. She was beautiful and graceful, and a favorite of the king, yet her people were facing genocide from a maniac. Her uncle convinced her to talk to the king, even though an audience with him at no invitation usually meant death. As she hesitated, she was convinced by her uncle that God had placed her there, "…for such a time as this." It was her turn, her time at bat, her moment in the spotlight. It was her time, and she was there for such a time at that.

We, too, have been placed where we are RIGHT NOW for such a time as this. It is our turn, our time, and our responsibility. Are you going to join us or take a step back? Do you see it and have you grabbed it? Responsibility is there for you at such a time as this.

A Slice of Life

I have been spending quite a bit of time on golf courses lately. It is an exercise in both pain and exhilaration. There isn't anything much better than standing on a green tee box with mountains in the background and friends around you. With the sun shining and the smell of freshly-cut grass in the air, being in the classic follow-through pose and watching a small round ball sailing more than two hundred fifty yards straight down the fairway is a wonderful experience. It is such a beautiful picture; something out of a coffee table picture book.

Unfortunately, it doesn't happen that often. It is something we dream about because we experience it so infrequently. I can hit the ball. I have hit it up to three hundred yards when I do everything right, but it is a rare moment when I do everything right. This is my normal tee shot: I address the ball (that's golfspeak for how you stand in relation to the ball), I measure my distance from the ball with the club length, and I run through the checklist in my head—elbow straight, hands holding right, head down, slow backswing, hit right, not fast. Then it happens—I pull the trigger and swing. I hear the metallic "chink" of a ball meeting a 105 mph club head.

Awestruck, the gallery gives a quick "Wow!" I look up to see my drive sail up and out 200 yards down the fairway. Then, the evil spin takes over at about 200 yards. The course of the ball bends and curves to the right, following an amazingly boomeranging trajectory, seemly turning 180 degrees and heading back to me. I find myself three fairways over, or I hit the fourth row of houses along the course. Some child will get yelled at because of me putting a ball in a pool a half-mile from the course.

We all dream of that perfect shot, and it only has to happen once in a game of one hundred strokes for us to come back the next time.

What is your dream? What are you working for? It's out there. If you stop working, stop improving, and stop trying, then your dreams have a tendency to get farther away. All I know is that my chances of achieving my dreams improve with every stroke I take, and my chances drop off dramatically when I stop swinging.

Am I Busy?

Life has started rushing by me again, and I have to ask myself, "Am I busy?" That may seem like an easy question to answer. In fact, it is so easy to answer that most people don't even ask it. You KNOW you are busy! But are we?

I am a nut for time management, order, and efficiency. Perhaps that came from my years as an inventory control manager and warehouse supervisor. I think it probably came from my mom. My mom was an unbelievably efficient manager; she could have taken over for many corporate execs today. Yet she confined her abilities to managing a farmhouse, husband, six sons, and two daughters. Imagine if you can the logistic nightmare of getting eight kids ready and in the car on time for church every Sunday morning. It all began early on Saturday when one of the younger ones would be given the assignment of polishing shoes. Back then, your shining Sunday shoes were an expression of your reverence to God, as well as a way to make the shoes last through the use of many growing boys and girls. I had that task for many years. Later on Saturday the baths would start. The use of showers was just beginning, and my father built one in our basement for the older kids and for efficiency's sake. Baths started in the early afternoon on Saturday with the younger kids, when our young mom would be able to handle two in the bath at a time, but as we got older that stopped. We would use the same water for two or three baths, since hot water was a luxury not to be drained away. We would call out that we were ready, and Mom would come in to inspect our ears, necks, and hair to make sure we actually used soap and didn't just get wet. Stop a minute and try to imagine the inventory of underwear that Mom had to manage for eight kids. It all had to be washed, separated, and stored by size. Underwear was all the same color back then, with maybe a different colored stripe on the band to distinguish that of different users. This effort had to occur with minimal battles among her young charges. Then came Sunday morning. Half the kids who were cleaned only needed a touchup here and there before getting into their Sunday best. The rest took showers, careful not to use all the hot water, and Mom herself would be ready as all ten of us piled into a station wagon for the thirty-minute trip to church. If space allowed, I would tell you about the breakfast management, the cutting of cherries to make sure all had the exact amount, the loaves of bread at each meal, the two-acre garden for food, the cow to be milked, and on and on.

Maybe that's why I have an inventory of unopened packages of underwear and socks in my closet right now. Thanks, Mom.

So now I stop and take a look at my life again and ask myself, "Am I busy?" I don't think so. I may have a lot of things scheduled and may have a "to do" list as long as my arm, but I'm not busy. My mom was busy. Happy Mother's Day, Mom.

Saying Grace

Thanksgiving is the one time of year when we stop and give thanks. We give thanks to God, to our country, and to each other. Thanksgiving is also the beginning of the "holiday season" leading up to Christmas and the New Year. We get together with family, we buy each other presents, and we smile a little more. It would be easy to focus this writing on how we should be thankful all year instead of having a season for it. It would be easy to focus this writing on how we should always do special things for each other and smile a little more every day. That would be easy, and short.

I would like to suggest that you give thanks already, more than you know. You do that by "saying grace." We "say grace" at meals, meaning we bow our heads and give thanks, but we do it more than that on a regular basis. Have you ever left a tip for a waiter or waitress? What you are doing is leaving a gratuity. The word "grace" comes from the Greek/Latin "gratia," and we use that word all the time in our lives. So when you leave a tip you are leaving a little grace or thanksgiving for that person. We are often GRATEful for something given to us. We can handle a problem with GRACE. Music has GRACE notes in it. When you quit a subscription to a magazine or paper they will send you a few extra GRACE copies. Someone who is good on his or her feet is called GRACEful. Someone could get into your good GRACES or they may inGRATiate themselves to you. Or, the opposite could happen. They could fall from GRACE or become "persona non gratia," a person without grace, or simply an inGRATE.

We say GRACE all the time, and most of the time we really don't realize it. It is built into our system and our society. We feel good about giving. Giving makes us feel good because it makes us part of something that is bigger than ourselves. When we give and when we say thanks we recognize the fact that this universe is made up of more than just US. We enter into a world where people impact us, please us, and do things for us that we sometimes don't even deserve. So in the holiday season and throughout the whole year, I encourage you to recognize your need to be a part of something bigger than yourself. You can be in a friendship, you can be in a family, you can be a part of a community, you can be a part of a country, and you can be a part of this world, something way bigger than the sum of all of us. Start small, and leave a bigger tip for that hardworking, underpaid waitress today.

The Fountain of Newness

A new casino just opened up in Las Vegas. It was in all the papers and on all the TV newscasts. A new round of casino advertising has begun. Many people came to the opening—celebrities, the wealthy, and the like. Many of them will never come back. But for something new, they lined up to get in.

I bought a new truck this year—NEW—for the first time in my life. I have never had a new vehicle before. I have gone through many cars and trucks, most of them started at a little less than 100,000 miles, and I added many more. I would run the tires until they fell off, then buy used tires that somebody traded in for new, and run them until they fell off. I saw no sense in putting new tires on an old, old car; they would be worth more than the car. I love the smell of the new truck when I get in it—the smell of newness. The smell of a truck that will work, will be fixed if it doesn't, and will look good getting out of. There is something about newness, but the problem with being new is—it doesn't last.

I can't really afford to buy a new vehicle every week to make sure the newness doesn't wear off. There is only one new casino in town, but it won't be new after I go there the first time. Some advertise a NEW restaurant, or a NEW game, or a NEW look, etc., but I have come to realize that even the word "new" gets old.

Personally, we do the same thing. We "ooo" and "aah" over a NEW baby, a new engagement, and a new marriage, or even a new graduate or a new job. It's that newness again. It wouldn't make sense to "ooo" and "aah" over something old. We want to bring that newness back to our old relationships and our lives. "Why can't it be like it was when love was new?"

Well, it can! I have found the secret formula for making what's old new again! I have found the fountain of youth for all products and relationships. These six magic words will revolutionize your life and bring newness back no matter how old and tired that vehicle is. Are you ready? Here are the six words: "Fake it until you feel it." That's right, I want you to fake it until you feel it.

Think about it. I just bought those handy wipes for my new truck. When it gets a little old-smelling, I wipe it down, wash it, and give it a little care. In other words, I fool myself into thinking that it is new again. In your relationships, like your marriage, you may feel like they are old and tired. Well, fake yourself into thinking that your marriage is new again. Do some of the things you haven't done since the relationship was new; give a gift, pay some extra attention. Fool yourself into thinking that you and your spouse are still dating and you're trying to win her heart. Keep doing this, and you will be surprised at the results! Even more surprising is something that for most of us is...well...NEW!

Back Pain, Cockroaches, and Getting Down To It

Life is hard enough without back problems. Life is hard enough without allergies and other ailments. Why did God create such a thing as pain? Why are there things like allergies and colds and the flu, or cockroaches for that matter?

A good friend of mine preaches a lot about health and wellness, and I have heard him speak about these topics probably a dozen times. He's a chiropractic doctor. He tells me that all these things are symptoms of deeper problems. He says that, basically, getting sick is your body telling you that it NEEDS something it is not getting or DOESN'T NEED something you are giving it. According to him, my back pain is not a problem (as much as it seems like it to me), it is a symptom. Pain comes from something. For me it could be that I worked my back too hard again (golfed twenty-seven holes, swung a pick for a few hours, shoveled clay for a few more, and worked, bent over a hole in the ground; all in the space of forty-eight hours). Or it could mean that I am simply twenty-five pounds overweight. A cold is your body working to get rid of some germs that got in there. Unfortunately, it is your nose and throat where you body has decided to dump the waste.

Chicken Little was hit by an airborne missile and assumed the sky was falling and life was ending and caused panic in the farmyard. He made his mistake by focusing on the symptom rather than the cause of the missile.

When Jesus was on earth he spent a lot of time stripping away the symptoms and getting right down to the nitty-gritty causes. The rich, young ruler had a hard time getting to heaven NOT because he was rich, but because he prized his wealth above love and concern for others.

As you mind your Spiritual Business, what do you focus on, the problem or the symptom? The symptom is usually easy to deal with; the problem is typically much harder. I can take drugs to be temporarily relieved of my back pain. That's treating the symptom. To treat the problem is going to take exercise, diet, and probably hiring someone to do the digging for me. Consider your pains. Emotional, physical, and spiritual pains happen. What are the causes of these pains? The sooner you find the cause behind the symptom, the sooner the pain will PERMANENTLY go away.

Remember Life

I have been spending a lot of time lately reading about cloning. Here in the United States, ACT Corporation has successfully cloned human embryos and human stem cells. If the current war wasn't going on, I'm sure this would receive more press than it has. But...

When I was young, my older brothers would send me out first to tackle my other older brothers. If I would just slow them down, the older brothers would take care of the rest. So there I was, a seventy-pound weakling running into a six-foot, one-hundred-eighty-pound-brother. Attempting to tackle him, I would more than likely bounce off of him and end up on my back getting stepped on.

Never being one to learn too quickly, let me try to tackle the cloning issue. First, let's try to define what happens. The whole process starts with the eggs from a woman. There are now people who make a business of "harvesting" women's eggs. Once you have some eggs to work with, you remove the genetic "material" from any cell from any person and you remove the genetic "material" from the egg and replace it with the other "material." With me so far? Now comes the tricky part, AND, I believe, the controversial part. The egg with the new genetic material needs to be coaxed into multiplying. Normally the trigger is a sperm cell working its way into the egg, but that would "corrupt" the genetic material of the egg. It would not be a true clone, only a fifty percent clone. So the scientists tried to change the genetic material of the sperm in the same way, but were not successful in getting the egg to multiply. So they studied what particular enzymes or stuff in the sperm and egg causes the growth and multiplying. They found the stuff and have a patent pending on it. Now they trigger the egg's growth without the introduction of sperm, and get a true clone of whatever you want—but is this a "viable" human life? The scientists say no, what they have made are stem cells, the equivalent of the cells in the placenta with the baby; the building blocks of life but not life itself.

Where do we as Christians need to stand on this issue? These cells can and will be grown into spare body parts and into cells for regenerating your brain (preventing Parkinson's and Alzheimer's) and into your spine (rejuvenating spinal cord injuries and cerebral palsy) and even into your muscles (curing muscular dystrophy and even aging), but the controversy is: Are they taking a life in order to prevent disease?

Here are my thoughts. IF the woman's eggs are stimulated to grow without the benefit of a man's sperm, then it removes the common argument that life begins with the uniting of the two. IF the cells formed are not the same as the embryo OF life, in other words if the cells formed can never grow into a human but can be engineered to form body parts and compatible spine and brain cells, how can we argue against it?

Our argument can be: "What will this lead to?" and, "They won't stop at that, they will clone a full human with the same technology!" I might even agree. But these arguments don't stack up against the benefits of this kind of medicine. To kill someone in order to save someone doesn't make sense, but to save someone even though there is a potential for abuse DOES make sense.

So in summary, remember life. That is the key: Life.

The Enemy of Miracles

Time can be your enemy in a lot of ways. No, I am not talking about the expanding waistline and the hair in places that I don't want and not in places I do want. That is just cosmetic stuff.

Time can take the uncommon and make it common. Time can take the amazing and make it normal. Time can take the miracle and make it the mundane. Time. Time is the enemy of miracles. Take a look back at a miraculous and amazing thing that has happened in your life. Back when it happened, it was the most amazing thing to ever hit you. You thought about it night and day. You told friends and family about it, and even strangers.

I remember when my daughter was born. It was night when I came home for the first time from the hospital. As I was driving along the expressway, I noticed a lady out of her car looking at a flat tire. I pulled over in front of her, hopped out of my car, took the tire iron out of her truck, jacked the car up, changed the tire, let the car down, put the flat tire in the trunk and was ready to leave—all that fast. She offered to pay me, but all I could do was stammer, "No thanks! I had a daughter today!"

The miracle of the birth of my children has been pushed back in my memory to the commonplace, to the mundane. Captured only in pictures, I see a young punk kid, too young to have his own kids—but I don't see the miracle any more, unless I look REALLY hard. Time is the enemy of miracles.

I am sure when you remember the miracles in your life you find the same thing, so what can we do? Two things, I think. First of all, force your memory, keep massaging it. When you touch someone, you feel it. But if you leave your hand on that touch, the feeling goes away, even though the touch is still there. Your hand gets "used to" it. To get the feeling back, you need to massage. Move your hand around and the feeling comes back. Do the same with your memories—massage them. Look at pictures, talk to those involved, and keep them fresh. The second thing you can do is to recognize the miracles of today. Appreciate what you have today. Look at a sunrise or sunset. Visit a maternity ward. Simply breathe.

Battle time as it seeks to turn your miracles into the mundane. Don't let it happen.

Don't Worry About It

There was a large article in the paper again recently about a skull found that was 1.7 million years old, supposedly the closest "bipedal" ancestor to a skull found in Kenya that is 1.9 million years old. There were theories on how this man migrated north into Europe looking for food, because it was larger and so needed more food than was provided in Africa.

I have often been asked about how I feel about these kinds of discoveries and claims, so let me summarize what I believe. Based on an exhaustive study of scripture, exogeting the original Greek and Hebrew texts, my master's degrees, my years in Christian Apologetics, my world experience in business and finance, and my over twenty years of marriage, let me give you my feelings and thoughts: "Don't worry about it."

Yep, that's it. Don't worry about it. Here's a little hint in interpretation of scripture. If it is important, it is clear. If it is something we need to know, it is not only findable but probably already found. We waste so much time debating and even splitting churches over biblically-unclear issues that I believe we are shooting ourselves in the foot over it all.

Is this world 6000 years old or 6 billion? If it were important Genesis 1:1 would say: "In the year 6573 BC, God created the heavens and the earth." What is important is that "In the beginning, God created." That is the thing to hang on to. Don't worry about the rest.

Will the world end in a few years or will it go on for a billion more? If it was important Revelation 22:20 would have said: "Yes, I am coming February 23, 2043!" What is important is that Jesus is coming soon, so we must be doing what we are supposed to be doing. Don't worry about the rest.

For more than two thousand years we have debated many different issues related to the beginning and the end of time. It is a fascinating discussion, but don't worry about it. Don't get so caught up in the discussion that you miss the important. Most of the time we work at answering questions that nobody is asking.

Don't worry about it!

What's On Your Quarter?

I am collecting the new statehood quarters. Suddenly I have become a numismatist (that's a coin collector to you lay people). I get a kick out of collecting. I am not sure whether that is a personality flaw or a hobby that takes my mind on mini-vacations.

I used to collect Hard Rock Café shot glasses but I got most of them; the only ones I'm missing are the ones that are really hard to get. So, I have been using my Hard Rock connections and trading my extra shot glasses for quarters from the different states.

Most of you have seen the new quarters by now I'm sure; they still have Washington on the head's side like normal but the tail's side has something different for each individual state. Some of the states held contests for the design, committees decided some, and some were commissioned by the state. There are many out now, all with different ideas on what to put on the tails side. A few have an outline of the state, some have trees, boats, birds, and airplanes. Many others are coming. I live in Nevada, and I wonder what we will choose in 2007 when ours is minted—a slot machine? A silver nugget? The Hoover Dam? Maybe Area 51 with some aliens!

What would you put on your own personal quarter? What is the most important event in your life that you would want everybody to know about? What is important to you? Your house or your job? Your kids or your spouse? The bank or investments? What have you done in your life that you would want to have immortalized on a quarter?

Don't worry; it isn't too late. You can still change what you have on your quarter; still change what is important in your life. After all, it isn't minted YET!

Making the Common Uncommon

I had the opportunity a while ago to perform the RE-commitment service for over two hundred couples who had been married for over fifty years. It was great to see them all together, although with a lot of wheelchairs and oxygen tanks. There was a couple that had been married for sixty-nine years. I asked them what their secret was. He said, "I just turn down my hearing aide at strategic times." She said, "And I know when he turns it down and that is when I spend his money…right, dear?" to which he replied, "What?" as he cupped his hand to his ear.

Obviously, one of the keys to longevity in marriage is a sense of humor. Many of the couples I talked to simply said, "We didn't give up. Kids today give up too quickly." Now that is some pretty sage advice.

I talked to them in my message about doing the usual, the ordinary and the common and turning it into something unusual, extraordinary and uncommon. They had taken their marriage, which is a day-to-day job that must be worked at. They had made a decision to love, repeatedly, over and over again, not just on their wedding day. They had put up with each other; they fought and came out loving. They had done all these common things for over fifty years, which makes them very uncommon. They did all these ordinary things of marriage with such consistency and longevity that they became EXTRAordinary.

That would be my advice to you as well. Don't give up! Continue to do the little things, the common things, and the ordinary things for each other. Do them with such consistency that they become uncommon and extraordinary.

That means that I am going to have to rub my wife's feet more. I am going to have to help her out with the things she is working on, and go with her to the things that she enjoys. What are the small things that you need to do? What are the seemingly insignificant things that will turn a rocky marriage, over time, into a rock solid marriage? Do them, and don't give up doing them.

I Did It—I Was Just Plain Stupid

My back hurts today, for two reasons. The first is that I spent my Friday working on the deck, hammering, carrying lumber, and generally doing a lot with my back—everything from bending over to hauling things. The second reason my back hurts is that I did all this without a shirt on, in the sun.

It is the sun's fault that I got sunburned. After all, if the sun would not have been shining I would not have this pain today. Or maybe better, it is the clouds' fault because they just didn't show up to create the shade I needed last Friday.

Really, though, it is my wife's fault because se gave me the money to buy the material I needed to work on the deck. If she hadn't have done that then I would not have had to work on the deck. Or it could be the workers at Lowes; they didn't help me with loading the boards in my truck, or unloading it for that matter.

My back hurts and I am sure that it isn't my fault. If everybody else just had done his or her jobs better, my back wouldn't hurt. I think I'll sue.

There is a lot of that going around nowadays. People are suing each other because, "It's not my fault and someone else should pay for this."

We hear it from people who spill hot coffee on themselves and blame McDonalds. We hear it from teens who go bad and blame their parents, from parents who go bad and blame the school, from schools that go bad and blame the government, from governments that go bad and blame the leaders, and from leaders who are afraid to lead because they will be blamed for everything.

Isn't that what we are stuck with now, leaders who are afraid to lead, and afraid to take a stand and call a wrong a wrong? Afraid to tell parents they shouldn't allow their kids to lose their minds to games, guns, and glamour. Afraid to tell schools that they aren't doing the job. Afraid to tell people they need to take responsibility for their own actions and not blame everybody else.

My back hurts. I was stupid. That's the end, and that's the truth!

A Note From the Wizard

One of my mentors, though I've never met him, is Roy Williams. Roy is the "Wizard of Ads" and author of wizardly books on marketing and, I would say, on life. He sends out a Monday Morning Memo every week to which I subscribe. This one fit so well with this book I couldn't resist getting his permission to add it.

How to Steal Your Life Back
(Or, Stealing Home Plate to Score the Winning Run in the Baseball Game of Life)

The catcher walked out to the pitcher's mound and everything came to a halt. Their brief conversation was punctuated only by the sweep of their eyes as they slowly scanned the crowd. The moment passed, the catcher walked slowly back to his place, and the game went on.

Later, the commentator interviewing the winning pitcher asked, "What did [the catcher] say to you when he came out to the mound?" The pitcher replied through a spray of champagne, "He said, 'Wow. This is it, game 7 of the World Series—what you and I have dreamed about since we were little kids. Now look up into those stands and think of all the millions of people watching you and me on TV right now. And every one of 'em is wondering what we're talking about.'"

Sadly, I'm not enough of a sports fan to recall the names of the players or even the year in which it occurred, but I'll always appreciate the wisdom of the now nameless catcher who stopped and seized a moment of his life for the scrapbook of his memory.

Have you been seizing moments?

Much has been written about the tyranny of the urgent, but I fear that very little is being done about it. Unlike that nameless catcher, most of us are swept relentlessly along by the flashfloods of circumstance and obligation. "Too much to do, too little time." It happens to the smartest people. But there is a subtle difference between a smart person and a wise one. A smart person makes a mistake, learns from it, and never makes that mistake again. A wise person is one who finds a smart person and learns from him how to avoid the mistake altogether.

Would you be wise?

According to numerous surveys, most people over sixty-five will respond with one of three very smart answers when asked, "If you had your life to live over again, what would you do differently?"

The most predictable answer speaks directly to the behavior of the catcher. "If I had my life to live over again, I'd take more time to reflect, and not push happiness always into the future."

Are you taking time to be happy?

The second most predictable answer among the over-sixty-five crowd is, "I'd take more risks."

Are you taking risks?

And the third most predictable answer is, "I'd do something that would live after me."

Are you investing your life in ways that will make a difference when you're gone?

The tyranny of the urgent will demand your life, one minute at a time, if you let it. Will you learn from these smart people?

Be wise.

Don't let it.

Roy H. Williams

Sign up for the FREE Monday Morning Memo at
http://wizardofads.com/main.htm

Momentum

It is college basketball time again in the nation. The sixty-four NCAA teams are primed and ready to go. There will be thirty-two games tonight and tomorrow and every sports bar in town will have a few of them playing on TV, all at the same time, all day and night.

I love college basketball. The kids try, as opposed to the NBA where I don't think they really try until the end of the season, then they step it up a notch. I love the sport, the game, the ebb and flow of a sweaty, funny-colored jersey'd dance that is basketball. I love watching team-work together more than I enjoy a superstar doing a high wire act. I love the slow motion replays of the behind the back pass threaded between the outstretched arms and legs of eight players into the hands of a wait-ing easy lay-up. I love seeing a seven-footer getting dunked on by a six-footer, and I love seeing the seven-footer protect his territory by swatting away any small guy foolish enough to enter it. I love basketball.

Basketball is a microcosm of life, as are many games. I could write for days on teamwork, coaching, defense vs. offense, the thrill of victory, and the agony of defeat. But I want to stress one thing that I see in bas-ketball that many don't see in life—momentum. When you watch a game you can see the momentum switch from one team to the other. While it is easier at a live game you can even see the momentum switch on TV. Announcers will sometimes tell you what you already feel. The team that comes from behind to tie the game in the last seconds to send it into overtime HAS the momentum. Even though a team may be behind, you know they are going to make a move, you sense it in the crowd's cheers, in the players' steps, and even in the bounce of the ball. Momentum: a powerful thing.

Momentum is like a wave that makes the highs seem higher and the lows seem lower. Momentum lifts you when you are tired, and carries you when you're too weak to walk. Momentum in your life is a powerful thing.

Do you recognize momentum in your life? Do you know how to build momentum? Do you know when you stop it? Here's a sugges-tion from the wizard of college basketball (not me—John Wooden of UCLA). Momentum starts and builds with unselfishness and is killed by selfishness. Wooden instructed his players that after they made a basket to point to their team member who gave them the assist. In other words, to give recognition and thanks to the one who made their basket possible. This small gesture gave that person a boost by receiving recognition for the assist by unselfishness, and started or kept up the momentum. When players think it is "all ME," then momentum is killed.

What kind of a player are you in your life? Do you want to get a little momentum going in your life or your team? Point to the one who made your success possible. Give them some recognition. You will boost their momentum and keep yours going.

Airhead in Life

I came home from a busy day of running around. Ten different lunch meetings, five breakfast meetings, a few in between and in the afternoon all kept the thoughts and ideas in my head swirling around like one of those shakable glass snowballs. I came home needing to write down the latest call information on my cell phone while sifting through the mail. I had two Gatorade bottles in my full arms—one unused and the other used and filled with my garbage so my truck would stay clean. After I finally got caught up with my day, I was ready to sit down at my computer and check my email. I thought I'd get my other bottle of Gatorade out of the fridge, but when I opened the fridge door I found only the bottle full of garbage sitting there, just chilling.

I had no idea where the full bottle of Gatorade had gone. It wasn't in the garbage. Someday I'll probably find it in my sock drawer or something. What an airhead! Did you ever do that kind of thing, or is it just me? I can find myself in a room with no idea why I walked into it. I find myself holding my cell phone with four numbers punched into it and realize I have no idea who I am calling. Maybe it's just me, but I find myself going through life trying to bridge the gaps in my memory by grasping strings just out of reach.

On an even larger scale, we all go through this. Do you find your days speeding by, with the months and years in quick succession? Are there things that you need to do but find that weeks have just gone by without you doing them, like sending that congratulatory card for a marriage or a new baby, or just sending a card to a friend, now years after the fact?

All of us have those times of being an airhead at life. We are told to "stop and smell the roses" and to "seize the day" and all that other sage advice, but life continues to go by and we continue to miss it. It's like trying to read the writing on train cars while you sit waiting for them to go by: you catch one but four more go by in a blur.

Stop and set your priorities. There is no way you can read all the train cars going by, so focus on the important ones. Force yourself to sit down with the ones you love, push everything aside, and ask them questions, even corny questions. I like to write down how my day went when I am traveling so that I can share it later with my wife before I forget. Without these notes I would open the fridge and find just the garbage instead of the stuff of life.

That's Just Wrong

I read something encouraging in *TIME* magazine this past week ("Why Did She Do It?" 11/18/02). It was an article on the whole Winona Ryder shoplifting incident. First the bad news: shoplifting costs all of us $10 billion a year. Psychologists quoted in the article state that teens shoplift mainly because of peer pressure from a dare of one of their friends. Adults do it more for the thrill of getting away with it, kind of like sky-diving or bungee jumping. But there is an increasingly larger group of people who compulsively steal because they cannot help themselves. They started doing it as kids and now the "pleasure fix" is needed.

After watching a store surveillance video with five different angles illustrating her kleptomania, Winona had the gall to plead innocent. Now wait a minute! Didn't you see the five different angles of you tearing off tags and shoving over $5,000 worth of clothes in your bag? And you plead innocent? Apparently guilt or innocence in her mind is not a matter of whether she did it but a matter of a state of mind WHEN she did it.

Now to the encouraging part: *TIME* tells of some of her influences growing up. She had a "loopy childhood in a Northern California commune with parents who smoked a lot of pot and chose Timothy Leary to be her godfather." She has continued to play disturbed, suicidal, and homicidal roles in her choices of movie roles. For *TIME* to connect her disturbing behavior to a disturbed childhood is quite an advance for the normally liberal magazine.

I am encouraged to see the pendulum swinging back to people taking responsibility for their actions instead of blaming everything and everyone except themselves. I am encouraged to see years of questionable thinking adjusted back to the need for solid homes and solid values. I am encouraged to see people realizing the connection between CEO's who steal and manipulate to a society without a moral foundation to anchor to. I am encouraged to hear people say again, "That's just wrong!

Bearing Fruit

Have you ever been close to someone who was bearing fruit?

Fruit is that part of a plant that lets you know that it is alive. Fruit carries with it the promise of a future within its seeds. Fruit carries hope. Fruit is visible hope and life.

Have you ever been close to someone who was bearing fruit?

I met a man with no fruit. We were forced into a conversation by being seated together at a conference. As he began to speak I found his words hung in the air like rotten apples on a tree. His words were dark, sickeningly mushy, and smelled. There was nothing good in what he said about himself, his marriage, his kids, and his job. There wasn't a ray of hope or life in his words.

Have you ever been close to someone who was bearing fruit?

I met a man with so much fruit I could have sat in his shade for many seasons. He talked of life. His smile was fresh. Hope grew out of him like a cluster of grapes pulling its vine to the ground. I passed by him only briefly but wherever he went he left people with a ray of sunshine like an unexpected gift.

Have you ever been close to someone who was bearing fruit?

Let's take a look in the mirror of our life experience. Do people want to be around you? Do you find yourself unable to get away from people for some "me" time? Do you find that you have people calling you their friend even though you would not consider them a friend? Or do you find that you have a hard time keeping what you would call "good" friends? Do you find that you are having a hard time finding someone to hang out with? Does anybody stop by your office, locker, or house just to talk?

Have you ever been someone who was bearing fruit?

Our House

Time magazine's cover story recently was on how homes have changed over the years as a result of recent and not-so-recent technology, trends, and world events. Dining rooms and kitchens have evolved into great rooms and breakfast nooks. Front porches have moved to the back of the house disguised as patios and grilling spaces. Making sure there are plugs in each room has been pushed aside by co-axial cable, optic phone lines, and communication wires. The hearth is now the plasma screen complete with digital flames.

For safety reasons the porch swing we used to sit on, swing on, and watch the neighborhood from is there no longer. The fronts of our homes become fortresses with surveillance cameras and stickers in the corners of our windows. We can go from our homes to our vehicles to our offices without ever going "outside" and into the elements. From the kitchen, Dad can e-message the kids that dinner is ready and their favorite shows are all lined up and ready with TiVo even editing out the commercials. Kids grab their meals and sit down to watch the latest shows or DVD in surround-sound and crisp, wide screen action.

Home has changed, and we might pine for the old days. We might, but I wouldn't recommend it. I think back fondly to the ten of us gathered around the kitchen table with the great home cooking my mom provided. The mashed potatoes, corn, and roast beef smelled like home.

But the truth we often forget when we wax nostalgic is that it really wasn't so great. My brothers and sisters and I would battle over the largest piece, and over seconds. We would battle over who got to sit in the corner of the table for ten because the middle two positions spent most of their time passing food and little of their time eating it. Mom would have to divide cherries in half to make sure we got equal amounts or arguments would ensue, and I don't remember a single meaningful conversation that we had at the kitchen table.

What I do remember and hold onto is the family atmosphere that made that house a home. I remember the love passed around between the arguments. Mom and Dad would spoon out equal amounts of concern, discipline, and love on our plates like our favorite pie with ice cream. I remember birthdays when we got to pick our favorite cake (mine was always angel food) and then blow out the candles to fun but way-off-tune strains of "Happy Birthday." Our family made our house a home. You know what? Even in the hi-tech secure houses of today, it is family that turns them into homes; people who love each other no matter what the circumstances and flaws.

I don't mind the shape and use of our houses changing, because the family stays the same, the love stays the same. I think what we need to work on is expanding our family. Welcome people, seek out new brothers and sisters, and don't hide from them. Be family to others and you will find your home full of fun and laughter and love, no matter how hi-tech.

Ask Not

It's a busy day, I have had four interviews with prospective employees already and the fifth is waiting in the factory break area. He sits there, relatively well dressed, nervously thumbing the pages of a notepad he has brought along. The break room is filled with posters of smiling employees and catchy safety slogans along with the brightly-colored chairs and white and chrome tables. I walk over and introduce myself; he stands to shake my hand, a good handshake, so far so good. I ask him if he wants something to drink as I walk to the soda vending machine. He sputters, "NO…ah, no thank you."Okay, I think to myself, a little insecure but he seems to be polite enough. I have gotten the interview process down to a few questions and a few non-verbal signs to the point where in the first five minutes I know whether I am going to hire the person or not. I am rarely surprised after that, but this young man surprised me. His insecurity really came out and he missed answering my critical questions almost completely, but at the end of every interview I ask: "Do you have any questions for me or anything you would like to say as I make my decision?"

Normally I get these questions:
   - "What are the working hours?"
   - "What are the benefits?"
   - "What would be my starting wage?"
   - "How long are your breaks and what is the overtime pay"
   - "I have a vacation already scheduled for this date, is that okay?"

What people don't realize is that the interview isn't over. They seem to relax when I ask that last question, thinking they've passed the test and now they can sit back. But this is one of my critical questions. This young man leaned forward, put his elbows on the polished table, held his hands out to me, and said, "This is what I can do for you: I will be here on time, if not early, every day. I will work through breaks if I have to, to get the job done. I will make sure that there is no doubt in YOUR mind that I have earned my paycheck that week." I smiled, stood up, shook his hand and asked him when he could start.

What separates employees is not how smart they are or how much school they have had. What separates them is their attitudes toward work and service. Do you earn your wages, or are you entitled to your wages? Do you go over and above your requirements and expect the rewards to eventually follow, or do you only do what's required for the money you get? Attitude separates employees.

It is the same in the volunteer world. Currently I spend most of my time in the non-profit, volunteer sector, and the most common phrase in that sector regarding attitude is: "I don't get anything out of it!" I am sure you hear it all the time too. No matter what the club or organization, you hear it. "I went to the Elks Club (or Toastmasters, or PTA, or church, or Big Brothers, or Walk for a Cure, or whatever) but I just didn't get anything out of it."

Let me give you a little help here. THESE ORGANIZATIONS ARE NOT THERE FOR YOU TO GET SOMETHING OUT OF! They are there for you to have an opportunity to GIVE, not to GET. If you go to these organizations looking to GET something, you won't find it. You will never "get anything out of it." You must go to these organizations with the attitude that you are going to GIVE as much as you can, and then you will find when you come home after giving all you had that something snuck in through the back door: a surprise, a gift of a job well done, and a feeling of satisfaction in giving of yourself without expecting anything in return.

Didn't someone famous somewhere ask this question: "Ask not what your country can do for you, but rather what you can do for your country." I think I heard that somewhere.

An Old End Table

This week I threw out a twenty-two-year-old piece of furniture. How do I know it was twenty-two years old? Well, I know it because I built it twenty-two years ago to be used in our first apartment together before my wife and I were married.

It was an end table and fit into a matched set of another end table, coffee table, couch and love seat that I built in the garage of my future in-laws the summer before we were married. The legs were built out of 4x4 and the tops out of 1x4. I screwed them all together and sanded them down smooth and ready for use in our new home. I applied a dark wood finish and sealed it with clear lacquer. All was ready.

We moved into our new apartment with shiny, new, handmade furniture in our living room (every thing else was hand-me-downs or garage sale items). Our small two bedrooms were soon filled with three of us, as a baby boy cruised around the end tables, banging his bottle on them for attention and for fun.

The tables moved with us to our first house where two more kids started pounding on them with their bottles. The tables were not just a place to put magazines and lamps, but also fortresses for Lego armies, homes for dolls, and places to hide during hide-and-seek.

Later years found them used for a TV and for small Christmas decorations. They were strong enough to sit on and used to launch assaults on Dad sleeping on the couch.

The garbage man picked it up this past Tuesday, dusty from over four years in the top of our garage, and did what twenty-two years and three kids could not…crushed it.

Dear Frankie, as I look back on those twenty-two years with you and our children, I find that our marriage has survived as well. We've taken the bruises and beatings of children, moves to different locations, pressure that doesn't belong and even spilled blood and tears from sharp edges that are now rounded. We have held up together, not so shiny and new anymore, but still strong and close. There are gouges in the woodwork that might not even heal with time but…you get the idea.

Now that I think about it, I probably should have kept that old end table, dusty and dinged as it was, and maybe given it to some newlyweds. Or maybe I should have put it back in our living room, that new fangled, particle board, table won't hold up to the inevitable abuse of…grandchildren?

I Think I Do

Somehow, somewhere along the line of history it was decided that Las Vegas was going to be the wedding capital of the world. Thousands of people get married here every month and tens of thousands every year. I perform the ceremonies for a very small portion of these and it gives me a great opportunity to study this phenomenon. Here are a few of the statistics I have picked up in my informal surveys so far:

- A full 80% of the couples who come to get married are already living together
- Of that group, 75% of them already have kids; many of them "stand up" in the wedding as the bridal party or groomsman, and even give the bride away.
- In 95% of the weddings I do they ask for a "religious" ceremony.
- 98% of the weddings are for people from out of town
- The two largest age groups for weddings are 20-30 and 40-50 groups
- The size of the wedding averages about 15—20 people, with a few 150 or more and a lot 5 or less in attendance.

I'd give you more detail but I think you get the idea of the flavor of the weddings done. Now I work at a classy wedding chapel, which tends to attract larger groups and wealthier groups. So I don't mean to say this is the Las Vegas picture, this is just a slice of the people I see.

There are so many stories of things that happen during the weddings that I am going to have to put them into a book someday. One of the most telling stories that typifies a lot of the weddings I see as well as weddings in general was the story of a young man. This groom was nervous from the start, but he tried to cover it by jokes and pacing. His bride was cool, calm, and beautifully collected. He stood with me on the stage as his bride walked down the aisle with her dad. After a little push, he went to shake his future father-in-law's hand and offer his left elbow to his bride. The two of them managed the one-step stage and were facing me for the meaning of marriage. They then turned to face each other for their vows. Both wanted me to state their vows and then they would simply say, "I do" at the end when asked. The groom was first, sweating and eyes darting everywhere but into the fresh, sparkly, blue eyes of his bride. When I finished the vow I looked expectantly at him. Lost in the moment, he forgot where he was, forgot the people, even his bride, and looked at me and said, "I think I do." Laughter broke out among the thirty guests gathered there, but his bride looked hurt. I went on with her vows and she responded with an emphatic "I DO," emphasizing the "I" heavily.

I would have to say that this young man spoke more truth in those four words than all the most eloquent vows that I have heard. Weddings tend to be a dream world of lovey-dovey, moist-eyed unreality. The real world of marriage hits you in the next few years. No one can speak with a certainty about the future in the way we ask on wedding days. If I'd have know the amount of work being married takes BEFORE I promised all that stuff, I am not sure I'd have done it. That is why so many marriages have trouble, no matter how old you marry or how many times or even if you live together first (which is another problem in itself).

Are you married right now? Say "I do" daily, do it today, do it tomorrow, and keep on doing it. It is a daily decision—not one that is made once and for all time. I have high hopes for that young man. Honesty is a good way to start a marriage.

The Sunday Paper

I have a weird quirk about my Sunday newspaper. No one may open it but me; no one may touch it, take off the rubber band or take it out of the baggie but me. I feel the same way about all my newspapers (three different ones) during the week too, but there is something special about the Sunday paper.

I like the crisp smell of the ink as the paper unfolds. I like to take it apart and read it one section at a time, then carefully place it on the floor face down. The read the next section and place it carefully on top of section A in a nice neat stack. By the time I am done reading it and place the last section on the neat little pile I fold it again in half and flip it over so that it shows me the front page, above the fold. I smile with satisfaction at the accomplishment, not only of reading a paper front to back but also achieving a nice, neat stack in the process.

There is not much that messes up my life more than my paper spread all over the house, crinkled and disheveled. My wife and kids know not to mess with my Sunday Paper. They can come in and tell me they just ran their car into the garage, quite school, joining a motorcycle gang or any-thing…don't ruffle me at all…just don't touch my Sunday paper. When my Sunday paper is handled properly then all is right with the world, God is in his heaven, and the sun comes up in the morning.

What is your Sunday paper? What is your quirk? Do you know it? Better yet, do your loved ones know it? It would be a great idea to let those around you know what that thing is that will set off your day right or wrong so that they can help you make sure it is right. If you don't, you might end up with your Sunday paper spread all over the house BEFORE you've read it (makes me shiver just thinking about it). Let your loved ones know. Also get to know the Sunday paper in the lives of your loved ones. One of your jobs as husband or wife or friend is to get to know those quirks and learn to avoid them.

It will be Sunday again soon, and I can hear the solid thunk of my paper as it hits my driveway early in the morning—nirvana in a rubber band.

The World's Richest Man

I just finished an article in *Fortune* magazine about the world's richest man: Bill Gates. First I think it is kind of cool that that world's richest man has such a common name. It's not Sultan Whatchamacallit, or King Whatshisname, or even Herbert William Zonkum III. It is simply Bill Gates. Regardless of how you feel about the company and the product, or even the way Bill made it to the top, you have to appreciate his current position.

First of all, Bill had a vision that proved to be the right one. He saw that the future of computers was not in the hardware but in the software. So at first when it was just IBM and Apple that made computers Bill played them against each other while he developed software for both. Then when all the competitors came in, and all the cheap knock-off computers pushed the big two out of the market, Bill was still there providing the software needed to make sure all the computers could do the same thing. He made millions, and then he made billions. It took him only twenty years to become the world's richest man. He screamed past the oil tycoons, the wealthy industrialists, the retail store magnates, and even the governments of eighty percent of the world. Now he is worth over sixty billion dollars and there is no clear ceiling in sight.

Bill was a lonely computer geek, driven by the need to win. Sometimes that got him into trouble; instead of competing he would just buy them and put them out of business. All the employees he had to manage and all the new products that needed a "Bill-look"were grinding on him. He was forty-two years old with no more mountains to climb. He became like Alexander the Great who cried when he defeated his last enemy because, basically, there was nothing challenging left to do. So Bill switched his life around and in so doing switched his priorities. He got married and had kids, so he started to come home at the end of a workday and on weekends instead of sleeping at the office. He took billions of his hard earned cash and put it into a foundation and started helping others. He traveled to Africa and gave money to support efforts in preventing AIDS. He went to inner city schools and gave them computers and money for better education. He stepped down from the day-to-day operation of a billion dollar company and put himself in charge of the creative "dream team" so he could have the fun at work he did when he was twenty. The *Fortune* article says he is smiling again, he is creating again, and he is loving it, which should have his competitors really worried.

Take a look at your life. Are you doing the things you should be doing to love your life? Are you in the situation you are in because you have to be or because you are too scared to change it? I know you don't have billions to do whatever you want, but you do have the capability to nudge your life in the direction you want to go. Do it today. Sign up for that class, start painting again, start writing that novel, start saving for that vacation, start planning for your future. Just START. It's a small step, but nothing gets done without STARTing.

A Slice of Life

I have been spending quite a bit of time on golf courses lately. It is an exercise in pain and exhilaration. There isn't anything much better than standing on a green tee box with mountains in the background and friends around you, smelling the freshly-cut grass, with the sun shining and you in the classic follow-through pose, watching a small round ball sailing more than two hundred fifty yards straight down the fairway. It is such a beautiful picture—something out of a coffee table picture book.

Unfortunately, it doesn't happen that often. It is something we dream about because we see it so IN-frequently. I can hit the ball; I have hit it up to three hundred yards when I do everything right. But it is so rare that I do everything right. This is my normal tee shot: I address the ball (that's golfspeak for how you stand in relation to the ball), I measure my distance from the ball with the club length, I run through the checklist in my head: elbow straight, hands holding right, head down, slow backswing, hit right—not fast. Then it happens, I pull the trigger and swing. I hear the metallic "chink" of a ball meeting a club head at one hundred five miles per hour. Awestruck, the gallery gives a quick "Wow!" I look up to see my drive sail up and up, two hundred yards down the fairway. Then, the evil spin takes over. At about two hundred yards it bends and curves to the right, following an amazingly boomeranging trajectory, seemly turning one hundred eighty degrees and heading back to me. I find myself three fairways over, or I hit the fourth row of houses along the course. Some child will get yelled at because of me for putting a ball in a pool a half-mile from the course.

We dream of that perfect shot, and it only has to happen once in a game of one hundred strokes for us to come back the next time.

What is your dream? What are you working for? It's out there. If you stop working, stop improving, and stop trying, your dreams have a tendency to get farther away. All I know is that my chances of achieving my dreams improve with every stroke I take, and my chances drop off dramatically when I stop swinging.

CHAPTER FOUR

Dealing with Demons

Can you feel them? Can you feel their icy cold tentacles working their way into your mind and into your thoughts? Those demons we all deal with hang onto whatever handhold you give them.

Remember that monster in the movie *Alien*? Sigourney Weaver had to kill that thing one hundred times and it kept coming back. The thing had some kind of handhold and was even reduced to one finger hanging on but still hanging on. Those demons in our lives are just as tenacious and just a determined. No matter how many times we feel we have exorcised them, they seem to come back.

Demons we carry are usually only known by us. Sometimes in the extreme others know them but that actually is rare. Rare are the extreme addicts to drugs, alcohol, eating, or sex. More common are those demons that we all carry, the smaller ones, and the ornery ones.

Early in our marriage we had an old house. I mean an OLD house, well over one hundred years old, and that old house had a bat problem. We told our kids those dark things flying around in their bedrooms at night were big butterflies. It didn't take them too long to figure out the truth. One night they came running down the stairs afraid of one of those butterflies, and as I looked up the staircase, the thing flew right into me and hung onto my chest hair. Ewwwwww! Talk about freaking out!

I finally got the thing off me and got it into a jar. I thought the kids could take it to school or something for science. But as I looked at it, it bared its teeth and started screaming (calling all its friends I think), so I got rid of it—quickly.

I'd like to help you get a handle on your demons. Let's try to put them in a jar and get rid of them—once and for all!

The Christmas Spirit

It's Christmastime and everywhere you look you can see the Christmas Spirit. Houses and trees are decorated. Presents are bought and wrapped, or at least thought about. I usually wait until the last minute but I do think about it a lot. Even people have the Christmas Spirit: they are nicer to each other, smile more often and even put up with the lines at the stores and the post office.

We talk about the Christmas spirit, but what exactly is it? We all know what Christmas is. Even those who don't know the child of Christmas know the event celebrated. Christmas Spirit is the general term given to this feeling of goodwill toward others and the sense of unselfishness overrunning our normally inward looking lives. Or to say it simply: We feel good and giving.

I would like to argue the case that we feel good BECAUSE we are giving. I am not a counselor, I don't believe I can sit down with someone and pick through layers of "stuff" in order to get at the real cause of what is bothering them. I don't feel competent or comfortable analyzing and probing. So, I tend to break things down to simple equations and come up with ways to overcome the issues in people's lives. That is why I think this thing called the Christmas Spirit is an important equation in our lives.

Humans tend to be selfish. We're all bothered by that demon. It is part of our nature to put ourselves in before others. Just watch kids trying to share toys for a while. I don't think we grow too much past the "THAT'S MINE" quick grab of toddlers. We just become more sophisticated in the grab and more refined in saying "That's mine."

The Christmas Spirit flies right into the face of that demon. By focusing on giving instead of getting, by focusing on goodwill instead of MY will we slap it in the face. We find that we feel better for a little while. To see the face of a child opening a present, the face of friends and family when the wrapping is crumpled in a pile. This Spirit battles that selfish demon by forcing us to give.

But I believe the Christmas Spirit translates beyond Christmas. I believe the best battle against selfishness, depression, loneliness and many other demons is giving. Get up and serve someone, work in a soup kitchen, volunteer at a hospital, or just help your neighbor. Giving is one of the cure-all pills for those demons that ail you. Take a heavy dose of it today!

We Don't Yell at Each Other Anymore

What is up with Halloween? I don't understand the whole concept. But it seems that if anyone raises any questions about it you become the Grinch who stole candy out of little kids' mouths. While I'm all for holidays, days off, and fun for kids, I'm not a big fan of Halloween. I think it is a symbol of something we have lost.

There was a time in America, and other countries as well, when debate and differences were celebrated and even encouraged. There was a time when Lincoln and Douglas yelled at each other in Presidential debates, insulting the intelligence of the opponent, and the audience loved it, ate it up. A religious speaker like Tony Campolo would go to secular campuses in the sixties and have tomatoes thrown at him for his views; college students would stand and yell at him during his lectures and speeches.

What does this have to do with Halloween, you ask? Well, do you know the origins of the holiday? November 1 was the Druid (nasty religious cult) New Year. It was celebrated as the Day of the Dead. People would light fires and dance around them wearing masks and consumes to fit in with the dead walking around. They would play tricks on the living unless a treat was left for them. In 834 AD, Gregory IV added a holiday to the church's calendar to compete with this Druid New Year and called it "All Saints Day." All good Roman Catholics were REQUIRED to attend mass. It was to be a celebration of the saints who had died. But with the druid influence, the evening before, took on a darker meaning: "All Hallows Eve," or the evening before All Saints Day that hallowed (holy) day. The cultic practices of fire and masks have continued...all the way to today's version of All Hallows Eve, Halloween.

Well, that was then and this in now. We don't dance with dead people anymore or serve the gods of the dead. Halloween is just a fun time for kids. Right? Even if we disagree, we would be out of place to say it wasn't. And so have not only tamed down our religious holidays, we have tamed down our secular holidays. We have tamed the debate out of our lives. We have lowered all debate to the lowest common denominator so that we can all agree, all just get along. Whether it is Halloween, Christmas combined with Hanukah, combined with Kwanza, or Easter with bonnets, eggs, bunnies, and such, we all go along to get along. This is why Americans were SO surprised to find that there are people in this world who HATE us, who are trained to hate us, and who will sacrifice themselves to that hate. "But we just wanted to get along," said the voice viewing the rubble with tears.

Maybe focusing on getting along isn't where we should be focused. Maybe, just maybe, a little honest debate and differences between us is just what the Master ordered.

Red Tape

I have been working with our local government agencies recently in an attempt to get a "permit" so that I can be "permitted" to do something in an area that has been "zoned" for something else. Now, getting this "permit" requires the negotiation of a myriad of red tape. Let me give you an example. In order to have my permit application accepted, I needed to supply a filled out application that was notarized and signed by the owner of the building, four copies of the site plan, two copies of the floor plan, two copies of the elevation drawings, two copies of the landscaping plan, a locator map, two assessor's maps, two zone boundary maps, two copies of the legal deed, a legal description, a parking analysis, justification letter, and if the property is on a flood plane, a drainage plan. All of this to get a "permit."

Why do I need the county's permission to be allowed to pay someone to meet on his or her property? Why are there certain things that are "zoned" out of certain areas while others are "zoned" into certain areas? Why do we do this to ourselves?

Here's my theory. I think red tape was one of mankind's punishments after the Fall. Adam and Eve ate whatever fruit it was and disobeyed in doing it. God came down, knowing they'd done it, even though they hid, thinking they'd gotten away with it. But God knew, and because of their disobedience, God said, "Thou shalt have red tape!" and He "zoned" them out of the garden.

Maybe we should go back to the early years in America when everyone lined up their covered wagons; someone yelled "GO!" and everyone raced to "stake" a claim in the wide-open spaces of the Midwest and West.

Anyway, after having my "permit" application accepted by the planning commission I then had to go through a "public hearing" and a "planning commission hearing" to actually be able to do what we wanted to do. All in all it was a two-month time commitment.

Red tape is a function of the Fall. Okay, so God didn't actually say anything about red tape, but we find now that, as a result of the Fall and our disobedience, we have all these rules and regulations to deal with. If people weren't so selfish and money grabbing, we wouldn't have to regulate them and zone them into certain areas. We have found the enemy and the enemy is US! There are still a few places in the USA that aren't regulated, but it won't take long for them to be zoned too. It's our nature. But I don't have time to get to that, I have to get back to my paperwork.

Bossin' the Boss

We had a board meeting recently and I was voted down. Do you believe that? Something that I felt strongly about and wanted to have accomplished was voted down by my board! Imagine the nerve! And it wasn't just a simple majority; it was all of them—against me! What is up with that?

Well, truth be told, that is the best sign of health in any organization. When the board is not controlled by the "leader" or "boss" or CEO, you have a healthy organization. In the May 27, 2002 issue of *Fortune* magazine, the cover story was entitled "Why Companies Fail." The story set forth the ten big mistakes for the failures. One of the main ones was

"Fearing the Boss." People in the companies refused to report any bad news for fear of the repercussions from the boss. Higher-ups would "see no evil" because they didn't want to be the bearer of bad news, and so the Board was dysfunctional, working with bad reports and data that had been doctored to look glossy. The fear of the boss crippled corporations like Enron, Warnaco, and Sunbeam, according to the article, to the point of bankruptcy.

Take a look at what is happening in the Roman Catholic Church right now. The church members never sought to question their leadership, and, in fact, were brought up never to question their leadership. Now there is a huge problem and there is no history or track record of accountability available to fix it. Priests who abuse are a minority, but it gets all the press BECAUSE we have always trusted their leadership.

Bad leadership is not a new problem. Not holding leadership accountable is not a new problem. But both are symptoms of a sick organization. We are all human, after all, and we all fail. And the Peter Principle—that every person will be promoted to the level of their incompetence—is alive and well.

So, as much as it drives me nuts not to get my own way, I am thankful that I have a board that is willing to stand up to me and say no. It shows health, it shows thinking for themselves, and it shows maturity. We need more of that in today's world, as long as it doesn't happen too often to me.

I'm a Nut

For those who know me, the title of this essay shouldn't surprise you. Most of you already know that I have a lot of "nutty" tendencies. But in case you didn't, let me clue you in on one of the quirky paths my mind tends to walk down.

Steven J. Wunderink   77

I am a time management nut. I cannot stand wasting time. It is like the individual sands of my life are draining away. I have so many other things that I should be doing that, when my time is being wasted, I tend to build up pressure like a whistling teapot. Surprisingly the DMV doesn't bother me any more. The first time I went there it did, but now…now I bring books, magazines, my planner and even a computer sometimes. As long as I know I am going to be spending three hours there I can use my time efficiently.

I have a book in my truck for whenever I need it. I listen to books on CD while I am driving long distances. I even try to learn Spanish during long drives. Yesterday, I sat in an office waiting to sign papers for an hour. It was only supposed to take five minutes to go in, sign, make copies and be out, but…they were not ready for us when they said they would be. We waited, and waited, and waited, and my water was getting hotter and hotter. My day was so tightly planned that I was already re-arranging it while waiting. My water began to get hot. It didn't boil because I purposely worked on keeping the heat down, but…I was definitely getting steamed.

I am an organizational nut. I like a place for everything and everything in its place. I have a place for my socks, my underwear, my suits, my shirts, my pants, and I can tell at a glance whether I need to do the laundry or not. I have a place for all of my tools so I can walk right up and get what I want without having to hunt to find it. I do some part time work at a golf pro shop, and I find myself organizing the golf ball inventory into shelves for Nike, Titleist, Strata and the different types from the same company, the most popular ones most in the easiest to reach places and the ones that rarely sell in the hard-to-reach places. I like organization and everything in its place. To me there is almost nothing worse than going to find something and it not being where it was supposed to be. That drives the organizational part of me nuts and the time management part of me nuts.

There, now you know a little about what makes me tick. The problem is: we live in a world of disorganization and of time-wasters. I am confined to controlling little bits and pieces of my life while the rest is too heavily influenced by the outside world and even my own family.

How does an organized nut live in a disorganized world? By dialing down the heat on the teapot. By recognizing how different we all are, that we are all nuts, so find your space to be you, in one way or another and I'll keep my neat, organized closet doors shut so the world can't see my folded underwear.

A Do-Over

Growing up with five brothers on a farm in Indiana gave me many opportunities for play, especially sports. We would play basketball, baseball and every now and again football. We didn't do football too much because the six of us guys would usually end up fighting more than playing. In order to keep the peace we would have to come up with an elaborate set of rules. Since there were only six of us, or even, at times, four of us, baseball was a little difficult, but we managed. When we were in the cow pasture, any ball that landed in a cow pie (if you know what I mean) was a "dead ball." In other words, you stopped when the ball stopped. If the ball hit a cow, it was still in play. Since we were all right-handed batters, the left field was "out" for the older brothers and the right field was "out" for me (the youngest), making it more difficult for the older guys and fairer for me. We had ghost runners who could only advance when pushed. We never played first base out; it was always "pitchers hand out." I think you get the idea.

Unfortunately, even with our elaborate set of rules there were still disputes. There were times when the call could go either way. If this happened, we called a "do-over"—in other words, everything returned to what it was before the disputed play. A do-over reset and replayed the game.

Don't you wish your life had a do-over opportunity? Don't you wish life provided the opportunity where you could come to your senses and hold up your hands and say, "Stop!"? Wait a minute...I want a do-over!" Maybe it is something you said to your spouse that you realized as soon as it was out of your mouth...you blew it. Or maybe, while backing out of a parking space, you hit the car next to you. Or maybe the "fun" you had last night turned out to be "not-so-fun" this morning. Or...you fill in the blank.

Well I am here with some good news and some bad. The good news is that life does give you a do-over. The bad news is that it is not instant; it takes a little time. We often think that we are trapped into the lives that we are currently living, that we are in a rut that we can never get out of. Well, guess what? You can do it over. You can be new again. The Bible calls this being "born again," but I just call it a do-over. It is a lifestyle change where you control your future choices, and your past choices no longer control you. It will take time and hard work, but it will get easier and easier with time.

Hold up your hands today and call a do-over if you need it. It might change the course of the game and maybe even your life.

A State of Indebtedness

You know what really bugs me? People who live their lives as if everything is owed to them. Just the fact that they are living and they have graced you with their presence means that they believe you should bend over backwards to reward them.

When I was the supervisor of a second-shift production crew, I did a lot of hiring. Since the jobs were lower level production, the people I hired would move on soon after their ninety-day minimum in my department. So I spent a lot of time interviewing new, fresh-faced applicants. Some weeks I would do over fifty interviews, so I got to be a pretty good judge of people based on just a few questions. I would basically ask them a variation on two questions. The first was: "What do you have to give this company?" And then I followed up by asking for examples. The second question: "What do you expect from this company?" This answer was then pursued by asking clarifying questions. Based on these two questions and about five minutes of a response to each, I could tell if they had a job with me or not.

Because during the course of their answers I would be able to see if they had their attitude right or backwards. You see, the majority of the people, both male and female, came in believing that if you gave them a paycheck, they would work for you. When the paycheck stopped they would quit. When the paycheck would not match the amount they thought they deserved they would complain, a lot, then quit. That is backwards and really bugs me.

The employees I wanted were those who wanted to prove themselves. Some wouldn't even ask me what they were getting paid or when payday was (the MOST common question of those who have it backwards). They would tell me that they must earn their paycheck and that they work for the love of working, doing something meaningful and helping others. They considered themselves indebted to the company for allowing them to work there. The ones who had it backwards considered the company indebted to them for deciding to work there.

Do you see the difference? I believe life would be so much easier if we could all remember just this one thing: to consider yourself in a constant state of indebtedness. If you do that, your relations with employers, spouses, friends and all relationships would improve dramatically. Consider that they owe you nothing and you owe them everything, then you will work to serve and keep their best interests in mind…and find your best interests will be fulfilled as well.

Turning the Hog

Back to the farm again. I find a lot of life's lessons were learned while growing up on a farm. My father used to raise hogs on the farm. Sometimes farrowing (birth to piglet) and sometimes finishing (piglet to market). If I remember correctly the ideal weight of the hog for market was around two hundred thirty-five pounds at that time. My dad would walk through the mass of pork with a yellow wax marker and put a line on the back of the ones who were ready for the market. The kids' job then was to sort out those marked hogs and get them up the ramp, or "chute", and onto the truck. Sounds easy enough, right? Wrong! Hogs are stubborn, mean and, well…pig-headed. They are also hard to handle. A hog is two hundred thirty-five pounds, with a center of gravity only a foot off the ground. I was a gangly, one hundred forty-pound weakling trying to convince this beast he wanted to go a different direction. We would sometimes use a piece of plywood with handgrips on it to corral them to the chute. We would have to crouch down low, the lower the better, and push the hog with the plywood, knees up against it. Even then, if the hog wanted to, he would just lower his head and flip the plywood—and sometimes me— right onto its back and just keep going. Even a club to the head wouldn't turn the thing around. It took planning, persistence, and constant attention to get the hog up the chute and keep it from turning around and heading back at you. It also took a lot of teamwork—my brothers, my dad, and I together getting all the hogs up the chute.

This came to mind recently when I was looking for a way to attach a picture to the concept of self-discipline. How do you picture self-discipline? I picture those undisciplined things in my life as a hog I have to get up that chute. What demon do you struggle with? Is it drinking, drugs, eating excessively, NOT eating compulsively, sex, or any one of hundreds of habits and quirks that pull us down? Picture that thing as an ornery hog that you need to get up the chute. It requires planning, constant attention, and persistence, and even then it may still flip you again and again. Plan to stay out of situations that will cause you to stumble. Give it your attention every day. Don't let it become "normal" in your life. Don't let it get away from you.

If that still doesn't work in turning that hog around, get a team around you to help. You can work with your family and friends, or even get a professional hog handler, but get control of that hog or you will end up in the hog slop as all of us did at least once on the farm. Always remember that it is not the one who falls who fails, it is only the ones who don't get up again.

Lifelines

I, like many others, have been watching the *Who Wants to be a Millionaire* game show. I'll admit it. I also am a *Jeopardy* fan, and once in a while I even watch *Wheel of Fortune.*

I have tried to call the number to get on the Millionaire show, not so much for the money as the fun of it. Yea, I admit the dramatic music and lights get a little corny after a while, and I admit some of the contestants take WAY too long to answer the question, but I still enjoy the show and it seems the hour goes by fast. I also have a partial list of who would be my lifelines should I need to call a friend. I have a sister-in-law who would be great at the artsy kind of questions. I have a brother or two who could handle sports. I have another brother for medical and science, and a sister who would take care of finance for me. I could field all the history or entertainment questions. I am set and ready to go, and I hope next time I call it won't be busy or telling me to call back later. I am ready; I have my lifelines, my dramatic concerned look on my face and, yes, that is my final answer.

Recently I saw a cartoon in our local newspaper. It had a picture of Regis facing St. Peter at the Pearly Gates with Peter asking him, "Is that your final answer?" Wouldn't it be great to have a lifeline at a time like that? We have all the important questions in life, and all the problems and demons we face daily. We have all the lights and dramatic music focusing on us. Now, at the critical moment, wouldn't it be great to stop everything and say, "I would like to use a lifeline, please."

Cheer up! We have lifelines available to us. We simply need to cultivate them. We have friends and family to support us in times of need; people who want us to succeed. Cultivate those relationships by spending time with them, by being there when they need you, and by being honest, open, and sincere. Those are the best lifelines you could ever have. So when you are facing the tough questions in life and standing toe-to-toe with those demons we all carry, call on your lifelines.

Pool Scum

I started cleaning my pool this past weekend. While the water was amazingly clear, the bottom was full of leaves and sand. I started out vacuuming the bottom and quickly ran into problems with the leaves clogging up the filter and the screens. I had to stop repeatedly to get the garbage out of the way. It was to the point where I was about to get angry with my neighbor for having a tree that sheds its leaves right next to the wall between our homes. They were all his leaves, why didn't HE get them out of my pool? Or cut down that tree! After nearly falling in a few times and cleaning the filter I finally got something done. Plus it was a beautiful day so…

I started thinking (I try to do that every so often) about the things that clog up my life; the things that I am constantly trying to clean up. I have many habits, sins, and quirks in my life that need to be vacuumed up. So, there are a few things that came to mind as I was cleaning my pool.

First, it is not an easy process. It takes a lot of hard work. Your habits and issues in your life are pretty engrained in you life and it will not be easy to get rid of them.

Second, it is not a quick process. It took me all day to get my pool clean. It will take you the better part of your life to work out the things that should not be there. Some of them are there on the surface and can be got quickly with a skimmer but many of them are in the deep end of the pool and it'll take a lot of time and patience to get at them.

Third, it's MY responsibility. It didn't do me any good to blame my neighbor for the leaves in my pool, even though they came from his tree. Many of the demons in your life were put there by others, but blaming them will not do anything to help yourself. It is also stupid to blame the leaves for being in your pool. "You stinking leaves, why don't you get out of my pool and quick clogging up my filter!"

Fourth, clean is good. This may be obvious or it may not be. Sometimes we enjoy the dirty pools of our lives. We enjoy our secret sins. We enjoy our habits. They give us an excuse for failing, and even an excuse for not trying. "No, honey, really, I love swimming in the pool with the scum!

Don't you? I don't ever want to clean those bugs out of the pool, they're my buddies!" In pools and in life, clean is good.

Fifth, maintenance is easier then startup. Once my pool is clean, it is so much easier to keep it clean than it was to get it clean in the first place. It is the same with our lives.

So come on over, and dive in. The water's clean and cool. My life…is still in process.

eBay Nut

I just got done spending time on eBay. I won't tell you how much time, but I will have to admit that I am an eBay nut.

For the internet-deficient among you: eBay is an online flea market. You can find just about anything you are looking for on eBay. Somebody somewhere has what you need or want and is willing to sell it. I have watched eBay evolve over the last three to four years for the good and for the bad. For the good in that it offers more and more items and the items are easier to find. For the bad in that retailers have gotten involved in the community and jacked up the prices. If you don't know your stuff you can pay more for the item on eBay than by running to a dealer. My favorite items to look at are coins (for my coin collection) and books on CD (my latest craze). I have also looked at everything from exercise equipment to Olympics tickets. Everything is there. Let's take something offhand: how about collector plates? Right now, there are 17,205 collector plates up for bid on eBay, starting at $1.99 and going to over $7,000 for a sterling silver early Tiffany butter plate. So, if plates are your thing, there you go.

I currently have a rating on eBay of 72. That means that I have had 72 positive recommendations from people I have bought from or sold to. I have seen some people with a negative number and they don't last too long on eBay because no one will accept their bid or buy anything from them. Many sellers won't even require that you send the money first if your rating is over 100.

I wonder what will happen when eBay takes over the world? It is one of the few e-businesses that have thrived and have proven that it can be done. It continues to grow and grow in people involved and items for bid. What will happen when it takes over? Maybe it would be convenient to have people walk around with their rating numbers on their foreheads. You would walk by me and see my 72 and think, hmm, he's involved, but not a really serious eBayer. I would see your rating at 2341 and realize that you are an old timer and that you were pretty reliable if I wanted to talk to you. We would both, of course, ignore the crazy guy in the corner with a −32 on his forehead. We could carry a screen on our front showing the items that we are interested in buying and on our backs would be a screen that would show what we have for sale and the current bid price. We would refer to each other by our screen names: "I saw Judy32456 had a 1924 Peace Dollar in MS64 condition the other day, did you get a bid in on it?" If we had a particularly popular item for bid, then just before the bidding closed we would have hundreds of people gathering around us to make sure they timed the last bid perfectly to get the item. We would…hmm…

Maybe the real world still has some advantages…I think I'll go take my wife out for breakfast…without even glancing at her current rating.

What's Wrong with Darkness?

I remember having to go from our house to our chicken coop to fetch some eggs, or to make an egg sale when it was dark out. Fall was the worst, the time had just changed, there was a light rain to make the ground and fallen leaves wet, and clouds still covered the moon and stars. I would pull on my shoes and my too-thin jacket to make my way to the coop only a football field away. At about the fifty-yard line I would start to feel it. That scared, kind of shivering, queasy feeling. I would look around at the bare trees reaching for me from out of the shadows, then down at the odd reflections of whatever light there was from the house shimmering off the leaves and wet ground like crooked eyes waiting for me. It seemed that evil lurked in the darkness, every creak and groan of the trees; every brush of the wind, and even the distant sound of animals turned our farm into a dark nightmare. I would quicken my pace to the point of running until I finally found the refuge of light.

So what is wrong with "darkness?" Why does it turn the common into the scary? Did you ever notice that in movies and in books that evil lurks in the dark? To the point that you can predict when and where the "boogieman" is hiding by the darkness around the heroes and the "dark" brooding music. You want to yell, "You idiot! Get out of there, you know it's in there!"

I believe that it is not the dark that is the problem. Darkness can be personified in music and literature. But it is what hides in the darkness that is the real problem. Darkness hides that which we don't want seen. Darkness hides our own sins. Notice the places where there is potential, or even kinetic, evil doings. In bars, in porn shops and strip clubs, and in nightclubs the lights are kept at a minimum to give you a chance to do your dark deed. It gives us the impression that no one can see no one and us can pin us down.

Light chases away that impression; harsh light in the eyes leads to confession and remorse (at least in the old police shows). Light chases away shadows and what lurks there. The same walk from my house to my chicken coup in the daytime time was a fun jaunt. We played baseball there, I rode my bike around the circle, and my brothers, sisters and I played in the trees. We played in the light of day.

In my reading of the Bible I find some unique connotations of light and dark. In the Creation story, while all God created was good, he never said darkness was good, in fact, he used light to chase it away. To the end of the Bible, when the end of time happens in Revelation, John tells us that there will be a new heaven and a new earth…and there will be no more night.

So where is your favorite place to play? Do you play in the daytime or in the night?

Just Do the Right Thing

I just finished up my taxes for the year. I had to get it done sooner this year because I have some kids looking to go to college and needing my tax statements for filling out the Financial Aid Forms (FAF). If I ever suffer from temptation it is during tax time.

I have the hardest time forcing myself to be as honest as possible but a straight forward as possible too. I don't want to give the government any more than I should but I struggle with giving them less. Especially now. The amount of scholarship and grant money my kids can get is dependent on how much I make, according to my tax forms. The less income the better, the more deductions the better.

So we run through the FAF and find that I should be able to give up to $18,000 per year to my kid's college education. SHEESH! Where am I supposed to get that? I don't have $18 K sitting in a bank somewhere! But you know, if I would have tweaked a little here and manipulated a little there, then FAF would have shown a lot less that I could afford, then my kids would have gotten more financial aid, then they would have more choice as to where they could afford to go, then…well you get the idea. Just a little manipulation for a really good outcome, right? How about this? If I get more money back on my taxes hen I can give more to my church and other charities. I don't have to worry about my finances as much and…well; again, you get the idea.

There are times when I can rationalize anything and almost everything to the point where I might even forget why I do the right thing. Do you know what I mean? I'm sure that we all have these things in our minds, habits and tendencies where we would just as soon NOT do the right thing. We all want to push the thoughts of wrong away and try to manipulate it into a way of looking like something right. I know, I'm there too—it's part of being human. But it comes back to you, wrong does; as many pieces of right clothes you try to cover it with, the wrong stench still comes through. It is simply too overpowering. When you find yourself wondering WHY you must do the right thing—just fall back on this principle as a guide for your decision making—JUST DO THE RIGHT THING.

Heaping Burning Coals

I have been impressed by the need to forgive lately. We talk a lot about retribution and justice, and rightly so. But there is something that we haven't quite grappled with yet: forgiveness. We talk about getting those terrorists or getting even with those murderers, even giving the death penalty to bombers.

I watch a lot of news and read a lot of newspapers and have yet to hear a serious mention of forgiveness. I would love to see the President, in his next address, tell us it is time to forgive. "NEVER!" I can hear the people say. "Not until they are all dead and suffering in hell!"

But stop and take a serious look at forgiveness. The biggest confusion is that when you forgive you somehow let the offending party "off the hook." Forgiving is allied with forgetting in this case. But that is not forgiveness. You see, forgiveness in NOT for the offender but for the offended. Forgiveness is NOT for the good of the one who hurt you, forgiveness is for YOU!

Whey you are hurt, offended or abused by another you have some chains that get wrapped around you. Chains of anger, bitterness, revenge and even sorrow. These chains keep you from living an ordinary, normal life. These chains keep you in bed with depression, make work and family seem distant, and they screw up the priorities in your life. Just think about the last time you were hurt by another and the emotions you went through (or are going through now) All of this anger, bitterness, depression and fear DON'T HURT THE OFFENDER, THEY HURT YOU! In fact, these chains are the offender still offending you from a distance.

So break those chains off you! You do that by honestly forgiving them. By going to them in person, or if that is not possible, get away for some quiet time. During the quite time write out on a piece of paper all the things that make you angry, bitter, fearful, depressed and whatever emotions that are tying you down. Write out the ones that hurt the most and keep you from living your life like you should. Once you have all that written down, a whole notebook maybe, or just a few post-its, take a match and light it all on fire. As it burns, in your mind go over all those things, forgiving the offender for each one, big or small. Release yourself from those chains and in so doing, really tick off those who think they still have you chained up, or as the Bible calls it "Heap burning coals on your heads."

Rolling a Dead Elephant

Spring is fast approaching and it is time again to roll that dead elephant in my back yard. It has been there now, this huge, stinking mass, seemingly bloating bigger by the week, for months now. I have tried to ignore it. I have even tried to ignore all of our visitors' comments on it. "Yea, I'll get to it someday." I would say, thinking all the time that I hoped it would just go away. Maybe if I ignore it long enough it will disappear. You think?

The weather got nice enough so this past week so it was time to tackle that dead elephant in my back yard. Before I started, I looked at the thing: a huge, smelly mass of vinyl, plastic and wood. Somewhere underneath the calcium crusted, dried mud, last year's leaves, puddles of brown water and green goo was my swimming pool. Last fall I noticed a leak but I could not find it. I even got in the thing when the water was barely above 40 degrees to find the hole—but to no avail. So I just let the water leak away, no chlorine, no maintenance and no swimming. No problem in the winter but now that it is getting nice out again it is time I tackle this dead elephant. I put it off as long as I could but…

So dressed in my scrubby clothes and carrying a five-gallon pail with clean water and a cleaning solution, I attempted to roll over this dead elephant. A few hours later, to my surprise, I found that it was not as big a task as I thought it would be. The vinyl cleaned quickly and easily. The bad water wasn't hard to get rid of, and I found the holes (four of them) quite quickly. Within a few hours I had it pretty much cleaned and ready for patching.

This dead elephant that I had been dreading for months was amazingly simple to take care of. A few hours of intent work and *viola*—the dead elephant has been reduced to a little mouse more scared of you than you are of it.

Isn't that the way with most of the dead elephants in your life? You know—those things that look so massive, ugly, messy and gross to take care of—a dead elephant. Once you finally get it in your mind to tackle them, they are reduced in size and scale to the point that you wonder what took you so long, what were you worried about anyway. Alfred Newman of *MAD* magazine always said, "What? Me worry?" which I believe is a paraphrase of the Bible, which says: "Why worry?" Who of you by worrying can add one single hour to his/her life? Or in my case: "Who of you by worrying can eliminate the dead elephant in your back yard?" Tackle it, take it on, you'll find it wasn't all big and scary as it was played up to be.

I'm Not Religious

As a lot of you know I read a lot of newspapers and magazines each day and each week. I like to see what our culture is going through and what it is thinking. I like to process the culture and see if I can get beneath the black ink at the motivation and thoughts.

The March 7, 2002 *USA Today* had an article titled "Amen to a Church-Free Life." Washington state leads the nation in a growing trend of Americans who say they have "no religion." Twenty-five percent of the state of Washington call themselves: "atheist, agnostic or secular" and don't believe in any religious affiliation. Most spend time with nature, family, or some kind of sport or activity. On the opposite end of the spectrum is South Dakota, which claims ninety percent of its people have some kind of religious affiliation.

I think what we have here is a failure to communicate, (to quote one of my favorite movies). People who tell you that they are not religious are telling you that they really don't know what a religion is. Let me say that another way. If you tell me that you don't believe in religion, then you have told me that you have a religion. Okay, let me try that again. I have had people tell me that they are not religious; they are atheists. Do you see the contradiction here? In essence they are saying, "I don't have a religion. I have a religion." Does that make sense to you?

Religion is the way we organize our belief system. Religion isn't good or bad; it is a tool to express your worldview. When you say you are an atheist that means that your religion is atheism, you live your life believing that there is NO god, or afterlife. When you say you are secular that means that your religion is one without spiritual beliefs but your belief is in yourself, or mankind, or science, or something like that. So don't tell me you're not religious, just tell me what you believe or don't believe and that will tell me your religion.

Most people seem to equate religion with church or synagogue or some kind of place of worship. These institutions have hurt many people, and religion in this context has become a negative. Witness the latest Roman Catholic Priest problem, or the Televangelist problems a decade ago. People in this article in *USA Today* and many other anti-religion movements lump these specific beliefs into a bucket called "religion" and speak against it. When really what we have are bad people in a good belief system, just as every belief system (including atheist and secular and nature lovers) has bad people doing bad things.

In that context I am not religious either. So I could be a part of the 25% in Washington. Let's not judge any belief system on its bad people, let's look at it by its merits...does it work? Does it make sense? Does it answer the important questions?

SERVE Therapy

I am not a counselor. I have never claimed to be a counselor. I got a C- in my counseling classes for my Masters degree. I slept through most of the classes knowing that I didn't want to counsel people. Having said that, I find myself in counseling situations weekly, if not daily. My job forces me to the forefront of people seeking counseling. Many in crisis situations in their life or the life of their family seek me for advice, comfort and a listening ear. So I have picked up a few things over the last decade or so. My tendency is to take a complicated issue and reduce it down to its foundation and address the core issue and not the surface ones. This tends to make me a little abrupt at times and even offensive at other times, but here goes.

I believe there is no emotional or psychological problem that cannot be solved by a good/honest friend and a consistent prayer life. Most psychologists and psychiatrists play the part of a friend or a confessee.

I believe that, at the core, all emotional or psychological problems are a result of what is on the throne of your life. "Healing" requires revolution, changing from a "bad" royal to a "good" one.

There it is...my counseling philosophy in a nutshell. I could quit now but I can feel the buzz of questions welling up inside you. "What about this..." and "What about that...?"

My first belief is self explanatory, but not easy. It is not easy to find a good friend who will be honest with you, confront you and still love you. It is not easy to have a consistent prayer life because it means being humble, admitting you can't handle situations and people and problems in your life.

My second belief is a little more nebulous. A simple question is: "Who do you bow down to every day?" Who or what is most important in your life. At the end of the day; who or what gets the most spaces in your check register? Bad royals on your throne would be money, possessions, a good job and even YOU! Good royals on your throne are: God and others.

I was having an especially bad day a few weeks ago. I was depressed, angry and focused only on MY wants and MY needs and MY time and MY pride. I stopped at Sonic to get MY banana shake with MY money and there was a mom and her daughter counting out pennies in their car next to me, trying to get an ice cream cone. As the waitress roller-skated up to me to bring my shake I asked her how much a couple of cones were. She told me, I paid it, told her what to do with it and left. For me, that was better than a month on the psychiatrist's couch working out my anger.

A Pimple on My Nose

Here I am, forty-two years old, and I get this huge pimple on my nose. Now wait a minute, wasn't that supposed to stop decades ago when my teen years ended? What is going on here? I can remember those years of waking each morning to see if anything had erupted and deciding on the best course of action to take if it had. I remember going to the restrooms at school to make sure nothing was embarrassing. Girls, at least you had makeup available. For us guys, we would rather have a bloody mess than the actual pimple. So here I am again. Of course it is noticeable; it's on my NOSE! My nose is big enough already without this huge protuberance to emphasize the fact. You know how normally you don't notice your nose, even though it is in your line of vision? Try this. Close one eye and look down at your nose. Do you see it? Well, now picture a volcano-sized red spot on the left side, so big it obstructs your vision. I have no depth perception right now because of this thing!

Okay, so maybe I am exaggerating a bit here. Maybe it just seems like it is volcano sized. But why do I have this thing? Well, medically, the pimple is your body's reaction to some kind of foreign substance on your face. It is a defense mechanism against infection and invasion; kind of like snot when you have a cold or vomit when you have the flu. Okay, maybe that was a gross analogy but it makes my point I think.

Why didn't God, in his infinite wisdom, make this kind of defensive reaction a pleasurable experience instead of a painful or even gross one? Or why didn't he just make it a hidden experience instead of a COM-PLETELY VISUAL experience? Instead of barfing when you have the flu, why can't we just smile and scratch an itch on our belly or something? Instead of having sinuses full of this gross stuff when we have a cold, how about our hair curling? Or maybe instead of pimples to expel the grime on our face, we just have our fingernails turn color? Then, the next time you see someone walking down the street with a smile, with curly hair, and scratching his or her belly with green fingernails, you'll know that person is having a bad day, but without all the mess.

Well, this falls into the same category as "If God is so good, why are there bad things?" God didn't want it this way and didn't plan it this way. We chose it to be this way. He knew pimples were going to happen but allowed us to make the choice whether or not to get them. We chose them. Along with a lot of other garbage. Just like right now, I can choose to take better care of my face or…not.

Meanwhile, I'll go back and check the mirror to see if I'll be able to see out of my left eye again soon.

Give Me a Break

As schools lean into the final stretch and many look to graduation I found an article on an English exam needed for graduation at many universities. In an article in *U.S. News and World Report* I found that in this exam all the offensive words had been taken out so that the exam on English Literature was now free from all gender, color and age bias.

So now, Mark Twain's classic *Huck Finn* had his adventures down the river with an "African American" and not a "negro" as in Twain's original. Hemmingway's *Old Man and the Sea* is changed to an "Elderly Man and the Sea". Jewish writers have everything that has to do with specific Judaism missing. Even in Walt Whitman's poetry the words "he" and "him" are changed to "hu" and "hum" to stand for all humans I guess.

We have gotten this whole thing backwards I think. Instead of working on ourselves we are trying to edit others. Think about it...wouldn't it be so much easier just to make sure that you are not offended then to make sure that everyone else doesn't offend anyone else? How can we judge what is offensive and what is not. We are trying to hit a target constantly moving. The amazing thing is that it is the "free speech" people who are advocating the "don't offend" initiative. Isn't that a conflict in interests? How can you possibly have free speech as a nation and NEVER offend anyone. I think I like the days when our politicians would get together and REALLY debate instead of dancing a waltz leaving us to decide who was leading in the dance. Back in the Lincoln/ Douglas debates, they used to call each other names and yell.

Let's not be so sensitive to offence. If someone offends you or burns you just turn the other cheek, walk away, consider the source and lets not run to the ACLU attorneys for litigation. Or we will lose classic freedoms and literature. *The Old Man and the Sea* will soon become "Somebody who did Something."

My Soapbox

I have to get on a soapbox for a minute here. I need to pontificate on something that really grinds me. So here goes.

I am sick and tired of lazy thinkers using the defense of "legislated morality." For instance: here in Las Vegas some government officials are trying to limit what can and cannot happen to customers at strip clubs. Now, the primary defense is that these are two consenting adults transacting business in a way that benefits both and besides, they say, "you cannot legislate the morality of individuals." I don't remember how many times I have heard that statement. And it angers me every time—okay, maybe anger is a little strong, but it really annoys me. I hear this argument in the abortion debate: "You cannot legislate what I do with my body and my morality." I hear it in the teenage sexuality debate: "We cannot tell the teens what is right or wrong since we cannot legislate their morality." As far as I am concerned this is a bunch of—as Colonel Potter from MASH would say— "Horse Hockey" or "Buffalo Bagels" or even a bunch of "Cow Cookies!"

Every law we have on the books of our local, state and federal government IS legislated morality! Maybe I didn't say that strongly enough: **EVERY LAW WE HAVE ON THE BOOKS OF OUR LOCAL, STATE, AND FEDERAL GOVERNMENT IS LEGISLATED MORALITY!** That is what laws are, by their very nature. What do laws do? Laws protect us from bad people. (Bad is a subjective, moral term). Laws tell us who is right and who is wrong (a VERY moral determination to be made between individuals) Laws tell us what the penalties are for being bad (morality? You bet!) Laws are often there to protect us from ourselves. (Also a VERY moral determination)

Take jaywalking; an innocent little law that we all break from time to time. The fact that "I can do what I want with MY body" is in fact limited by not being able to cross the road where I want to. The penalty may be a warning, a fine, or being run over by a car. Take murder itself. Who says when murder is murder or justifiable homicide, or self-defense or even war? We legislate the morality of death. We legislate the morality of stealing, of causing pain, of even using our voice to slander, cause riots and even yelling "fire" in a theater. Every law we have is legislated morality.

Anybody who uses that to debate a new law or regulation you can automatically tell that they are a lazy thinker. They are using words to manipulate others and not to debate. That is why the good people of the world MUST enter the public debate on issues and laws, or the "bad" people and the lazy thinkers will determine the morality of our nation. There, I said my piece; hope I don't fall getting down off this soapbox. I might have to sue.

We've Lost the Firewall

There was another incident this week where parents went crazy at their kids sporting events. Recently there was a man killed at a hockey game because his son did something to the son of the man who killed him. Now an argument grew into a fight and the fight grew into a brawl.

We've lost the firewall in our society.

A firewall is a last line of protection against danger. You have a firewall behind the dashboard of your car. You have a firewall in the ceilings of businesses and you have a firewall to protect you from bomb tests. You have firewalls all over your life. But we have lost the firewall in our society.

When you have to fear going to a youth sporting event because you might get beat up or worse. When you have to fear for your kids going to games, not just because of other kids but also because of the parents of other kids. When you fear for your kids simply going to school. When you fear to pump gas. When you roll up your windows in your car in certain neighborhoods. When you have to pass through security gates to get to your home, lock your car when you leave it in your garage, unlock two to three locks to get into your house, turn off the security system that is beeping at you and then check on your kids to make sure they are home safe—you know, we have lost the Firewall in our society.

So what is that Firewall we have lost? What specifically is it? Take a look at the last 40 years in America and you can easily see what we have lost…we have lost our love of each other. That love was our firewall. Not a passionate, hugging and kissing kind of love, but a love that respects your neighbor and his/her property. A love that makes the decision to do unto them as you would have them do unto you. I believe that love is embodied in what we call the Ten Commandments. I don't think that it is a coincidence that when we pulled God and the Ten Commandments out of schools, those same schools became unsafe places for our kids. Those kids, in the last forty years, have grown into parents without that firewall who beat on each other at kid's football games. Those same kids have grown into parents who now can't figure out why someone would have no problems "doing to" their kids whatever they want.

We've lost the firewall in our society. Let's bring it back…aren't you tired of all the locks that only serve to keep YOU in?

Living Life to a Soundtrack

I have to confess that one of the things I do that drive my wife nuts is…singing under my breath. Yea, I'm sure there is many other things I do that drives her crazy but singing is one that I am aware of. We can be riding in the car and she will hear me whispering to myself. She will say, "What?" And I will, again, have to answer, "Nothing, I was just singing." I wake up in the morning with songs playing in my head and me singing along to them. Sometimes happy songs and sometimes not so happy. What really freaks me out is when I am walking along singing a song and then I come into earshot of a radio playing the same song I am singing—like my mind hears it before I am aware of it and starts me singing.

I have music playing when I work at home, in my office and driving in between the two. I would even have music playing while I am watching TV but my wife stopped that. I live my life to a soundtrack.

I also find out that the music playing in my head reflects the way I am feeling. I might even change the station to try to work on my attitude. Change from depressing songs about death, leaving and pain to happy songs about love and fun. Sometimes it works and sometimes I have to put a CD in to help the change along.

What is the soundtrack of your life? We all have CD's playing in our minds. Sometimes the CD plays stories from your past—painful stories. Sometimes the CD plays joyful stories of love and friendship. Sometimes the CD is stuck on one track that tells you that you are "No Good," and "Nobody Loves You," and "You're not good enough!" (Those are #1 best sellers, unfortunately) What is the soundtrack of your life?

Don't like it? Change the station. Changing the station is easy to say, but sometimes very hard to do. Changing the station might even require the help of a professional DJ. But you CAN change it…in fact…that is what our God specializes in.

CHAPTER FIVE

Made in God's Image

People try to tell us all the time that we are no more than a bunch of genetic code that can be deciphered and used, sold and reconfigured. People try to tell us that we are only 1 percent different than apes—our closest evolutionary cousins. People try to tell us that we are no different than other "living" things and that "trees are people too." People try to tell us that we are just one lonely planet in a universe of billions and billions of potentially earthlike planets with potential other living beings, or else "it would be a awful waste of space." People tell us…you fill in the blank.

I'm here to tell you that we are different; there is something different about us. Something that makes us unique and even blessed above all other things. What is that? Some call it a soul or a spirit but then "they" tell us trees have a spirit and a soul as well—so what is the difference?

I call this being "created in the image of God." I call it that because the book of Genesis in the Talmud, Koran and Bible supports and calls it that. That is what makes us unique, different, separate and "holy" (holy literally means to be separate)

Let's look at a few of those things that make us different.

Raw Oysters, Mt. Everest, and God's Image

I read a book this past week called *Ghosts of Everest*. It was a book about an expedition in 1999 to find George Mallory on Mt. Everest. George

Mallory put together the first expeditions from England to reach the summit of Mt. Everest in the 1920s. Mallory was said to have coined the phrase "because it's there" when asked why he wanted to climb Mt. Everest. In 1924 he and a man named Irvine set off towards the summit and never came back. There was much speculation as to whether they actually made it or not, it became more than speculation, it became a national obsession until New Zealander Sir Edmund Hillary and Sherpa Tensin Norgay reached the summit in 1953.

Since that time the North Face has been closed to explorers because it is in China. A group from China reached the summit in 1960 and claimed to find the body of an Englishman. The authors finally got permission and financial support to climb the North Face of the mountain, and in 1999, climbed. They actually found the body of Mallory almost by accident. The body the Chinese found must have been Irvine. They found letters, food and his body perfectly preserved in the cold at about 27,000 feet. They found one of his oxygen tanks on the "Third Step" which was only a few hundred feet from the summit. They found nothing to prove or disprove his making the summit almost 30 years before Hillary, except for something missing—a picture of his wife was not in his pockets. He had promised to leave the picture on the summit when he reached it.

Mt. Everest doesn't hold the mystique that it did seventy-five years ago. It has been climbed so many times now it doesn't even make news any more. But what would drive a man like Mallory, Irvine, and Hillary? What is it in us that craves a challenge? What is it in us that craves conquering the unconquered, beating the unbeatable, doing the undoable? Whatever it is—our society NEEDS it. Without it America would never have been discovered, the moon never walked on, or oysters never tasted (think about that last one for a while, eww!). All the advances in our culture happen when we dive into the unknown and attempted the never-been-done.

I like to think that this is what the Bible call "being created in God's image"—that craving and drive in us is that part of God in us that separates us from animals and trees. I mean think about it. Wouldn't one of the most remarkable daring acts in history be the creation of a people, who might turn on you, spit in your face, fly airplanes into buildings and deny you even exist? But also these same creatures will love beyond reason, give beyond ability, create amazing beauty and even overcome nature to stand on a peak almost six miles (29,028 ft) above sea level!

God Smiles

I have a truth that I want to pass along to you. Here it is: People enjoy giving. There you are. Profound, is it not?

Not too earth-shattering, you say? I am sorry that I could not come up with something more astounding than that. But did you ever stop and use this principle, or really consider what it means?

People enjoy giving. Why? I know that there are a lot of people out there who enjoy getting too, but people enjoy giving. There is something about giving to someone who needs it, or to someone who doesn't expect it, that does the heart good. We enjoy it when our hearts feel good. I believe that it is a part of what it means to be created in God's image. It is something that separates us from all other creation. We enjoy giving. God made us, breathed life into us, and sat back and smiled. But what makes him smile even more is when he has the opportunity to give to us. In fact, the Bible says that he is looking around, searching intently for the person on who he can shower some blessing for a while; that person who is in need or that person who simply doesn't expect it. I can just picture God focusing on the single mother who is wondering where her next meal is coming from, and then he moves in the head of you or me to bring over some food or a gift certificate, or offer her a job. The mom tells you when you stop how amazing it is that you brought it over today, since they just ran out of food. You get a hug, tears are shed by her and by you, AND God smiles.

People enjoy giving. Allow people to give to you. Sometimes the hardest thing is to accept a gift, even when you need it. Don't be ashamed. Accept it, knowing that the heart of the person giving it is being infused with joy by a smiling God, and also knowing that you will be able to give back again, soon.

People enjoy giving because God enjoys giving. God uses us as his tools for giving. In fact, I would dare say that he blesses you so that you can bless others. He gives to you so that you can give to others. We receive the joy, they receive the needed gift, and God smiles.

Bad Things

So why do bad things happen? If there were a God, why would he allow bad things to happen to good people, or to anyone for that matter? If there is a God, he cannot be good. If there are bad things, if God is good then he surely cannot be all-powerful or he would not allow the bad things to happen unless he was powerless to prevent them. Have you ever had these questions run through your mind? I have. Often. So let me try to tackle these thoughts. Now, mind you, theologians and philosophers have been debating these issues as long as time itself, so if my answers don't satisfy you, sorry.

What separates us from animals? Our reasoning ability, our creative ability, our social ability, the fact that we feel guilt, etc. While some people try to tell us that certain animals have some primitive aspects of these qualities, it is usually a stretch to meet someone's own agenda. In religious circles this is called being created in the "image of God." He breathed life into us and he didn't breath that life into ANY other part of his creation.

Another part of the image of God is the fact that we can overcome our instincts with reason. Dogs are driven by instinct to eat, drink, and procreate but not humans. While humans need to eat, drink, and procreate we can overcome this instinct or drive with reason. We can choose to not eat, or even to eat too much when the body really doesn't need the nourishment. This is called free will. Free will is the ability to overcome our drives and instincts with reason and thought. It is a great thing that God has given us but it is also a potentially bad thing. Our free will means that we can chose to eat or not to eat, to work or not to work, even though those things may hurt us in the end. We can choose what is bad for us, even though our instincts tell us we shouldn't.

We humans took the "very good" part of creation—"free will"—and made it instead a license for doing all kinds of things that are bad for us. We chose bad, we choose bad and for God to eliminate that would mean he takes away that part of his image that makes us different from animals. We cannot have one without the other. To be made in God's image is to be made with free will. We cannot have one without the other and that means that bad and "evil" can and does enter our world.

But we want license without guilt. We want the ability to choose whatever we want and have none of it called "bad."

Fire can be used for beautiful things. It can mold and craft, keep us warm, and light our world. But it can also be destructive. How can we yell at God for creating the fire that destroys without also eliminating the fire that creates beauty? We must control the fire of free will and turn it into the thing of beauty that it was intended to be and not the destructive force it can be.

Bad Things II

I can hear a lot of you yelling at me now about the previous page: "I don't ALWAYS choose to be bad and still bad things happen!"

You are right. Sometimes bad things happen to you without you choosing the bad through your lifestyle or through your free will.

You see, it is my belief that the world has been corrupted by our bad choices so that now there is a momentum of bad happening. Take alcoholism for instance. Now there is nothing wrong with alcohol. What is wrong is the abuse of alcohol. So follow my thinking here a minute and see if I can explain what I mean by a momentum of bad.

A man, by his own choice, takes to drinking, and drinking a lot because he likes the feel of being drunk more than being sober. This generates a lifestyle of chaos. His wife is the subject of abuse because she doesn't want him drunk, doesn't want him wasting their money, and doesn't want him to die in a drunk driving accident. The kids are scared of him and the family is broken. Ten years later, what is the result? The wife was abuse and left him, the children are angry and also turn to alcohol and drugs, and the man kills while drinking and driving. It all started with one man who chose to drink, and it ended with many families and even generations of families affected—a momentum of bad.

So bad things happen because you choose them. Bad things happen because you have been caught up in a world where bad choices have created a momentum of bad AND bad things happen for two more reasons.

Bad Things III

It is hard to believe for a lot of people, but there is actually a living being out there who doesn't want you to succeed. Now, I am not talking about your boss or your in-laws. I am talking about a spiritual Evil, with a capital "E." A devil. This being goes by many names: Satan, Lucifer, Beelzebub, Lord of Darkness and many others. Why is this so hard for people to believe? We have no problem believing that there are good spiritual beings like angels or even aliens or "advanced" beings of some kind so why not bad?

According to C.S. Lewis in his book *The Screwtape Letters*, there are two "equal and opposite errors into which our race can fall about devils, one is to disbelieve in their existence and the other is to feel an excessive and unhealthy interest in them." Most Americans fall into the first category. But if you believe in God and his angels, you have to believe in the dark angel.

Apathy is the best weapon of Satan and NOT possession as is popularized by movies like *The Exorcist*. Satan "whispers" in your ear with temptations directed at you and you alone. He is called the "father of lies" because that is his sword. He cannot handle the truth, so that is our best weapon against him.

While this reason for bad things happening is hard to swallow, it is consistent and logical.

But there is one more reason bad things happen.

Bad Things IV

You thought that last one was hard to swallow, here's another, more radical idea for bad things. Bad things happen to push you toward change. Bad things happen to promote good outcomes. How's that for radical?

When I entered high school I had two things on my mind: basketball and girls—in that order. During my sophomore year I was dating the best-looking girl in our class, and I was the star of our basketball team. During a game I leaped up to catch a pass while running, and I came down wrong on my leg and twisted my knee into a mess of tendons and muscles. While I was in the hospital for my first knee surgery that next week my girlfriend dumped me. That was a bad thing. So, two bad things crushed my young life in high school. But as I look back, I see that those were some of the best things that ever happened to me. I grew in ways and talents that I never knew I had, and I developed leadership abilities that never would have been there if the accident hadn't happened. I was changed for the better.

Part two of my life story is similar and maybe you can relate. I was a fast climbing executive in a Fortune 500 company. I was working sixteen hours a day, and achieving things no other young executive was doing. Then, a new manager came to town and wanted to put his own people into the key positions. He told the rest of us to "start looking for other employment." What happened to the sixteen-hour days I put in? What happened to my blood and sweat for this company? What did happen was that I started spending more time with my wife and my kids and looking for a job that would include them instead of excluding them from my life. A bad thing turned out to be good for me and my family—very good.

So if you are in a bad situation right now, you need to look at it in the light of why it has happened. Is this bad thing happening because of bad choices you have made? Change your choices, even if it means you have to humiliate yourself. Is it because you have been caught up in a momentum of bad? Stop the Ferris wheel and get off, NOW! Bad things may happen because there is a strong evil in the world trying to get you to stumble. Then get outside help. Finally, bad things may be happening because you need to change, to move on, and to be a better person. If so, recognize this, and CHANGE!

Madame Tussauds

My wife and I recently went out to the Madame Tussauds Wax Museum in Las Vegas. It was fun. We got in for half price (always a good thing), and were immediately met by Jerry Springer. After we went in we could stand by Nicholas Cage, Sylvester Stallone, and Arnold. Most of them looked amazingly real; some not too. Mel Gibson looked like he was suffering from a bad facelift, and Kenny Rogers looked like someone had squooshed his head, but Whoopie Goldberg looked so real you had to laugh, and she was amazingly short. Then I came to the captain of the Starship Enterprise, Jean Luc Picard, or Patrick Stewart. He was so lifelike it gave me the creeps. I would go right up to him, nose to nose, and it was almost scary because at any time I thought he would startle me with a "boo!" As I looked closely at him/it, I could swear I saw him breathe. Weird.

Then we walked through the rest of the Venetian Hotel and Casino and the shops there. All over the mall area were "performance" artists. Some were contortionists, some were comedians, and some were living statues. The living statues were amazing. They were all white, wearing long robes, turbans, gloves, and they all had pasty white faces. They would stand immobile for hours at a time, even with people coming up to them and having their pictures taken with them, with kids taunting them and throwing things at them. One guy in particular was incredible; like stone!

What a contrast. A wax figure looking so real you thought it breathed, and a human looking so statue-like you couldn't see him breathe.

Those of you who know me probably know where I am going with this. In the Bible, God took some clay and formed it into a figure at the beginning of time. He then performed mouth-to-mouth, breath-to-breath resuscitation on it. No longer was mankind a lump of clay; it was a living, breathing person. No scientist will be able to that—EVER. Nor can we indefinitely hide the fact that we are humans and not statues. The more closely you are looked at the more human you become. What makes the difference between humans and wax or clay? Breath—the breath of life. The literal translation for "spirit" is breath. We are different. We have the spirit in us; the breath in us, and THAT makes all the difference.

Life in a Fish Tank

There has been an amazing amount of death in the last few months—mud slides killing people in Central America, earthquakes in India, floods all over, famine, and now we have the whole World Trade Center thing going on, along with the war that followed.

Back in my office in Michigan I had a fish tank. I had to clean the thing periodically, which meant I would have to shake up the entire world of the fish. To vacuum up the garbage I had to upset the rocks, gravel, and other stuff that I had in the tank. The filter would be working overtime cleaning the water that was now murky. I would drop the water level and add new water and scrub the sides of the tank. By the time the dust settled (literally), I would have a few of the less-hardy fish floating at the top—upside down. The fish tank had gone through its very own natural catastrophe, complete with earthquakes, storms, and the "hand of god" changing their world.

So what did the fish do? Well, the remaining fish got together and tried to save the injured fish. In fact, fish from other tanks sent medical help and fish food to my tank in support of the injured and traumatized fish. They formed the FISH alliance (Fish In Supporting Help) and raise money from other fish tanks to support my fish. Before I knew it, my fish tank was completely put back together and I had a thriving fish population!

Okay, that really isn't what happened. In fact, when my fish were injured, the healthy fish ate them. They wouldn't be floating on top for too long before they simply disappeared; many were eaten while still alive. I don't believe any fish in other tanks even knew about the tragedy.

When I want a simple example of what it means to be created in God's image, I need only look at the response to tragedy in our world. WE RESPOND! We don't eat our injured, we help them, support them, and lift them up. No matter what some loonies may tell you, we are not animals or even close to animals. We are men and women created in the image of God, and that makes all the difference.

Science and Sex

I read in the paper today that scientists don't quite understand the "pay-off" of sex. They say it is "not an efficient way to reproduce." The article goes on to say, "It is clearly one of the most fundamental questions in evolutionary biology." Asexual reproduction is so much more efficient in an evolutionary environment because one hundred percent of the "good" chromosomes go into the next generation, whereas only fifty percent of the "good" go into sexual reproduction and the other fifty percent may be questionable. Then, after reproduction, only half the results have a womb, which cuts the reproductive capacity in half. Males apparently just clog up the evolutionary works.

Now I don't know who these scientists are—most of them are from the University of California at Santa Barbara—but GIVE ME A BREAK!

You don't know what the payoff of sex is? That is probably one of the most ridiculous statements I have ever heard. This is evidence to me of evolutionary biology run amuck. When you deconstruct a human down to a series of chromosomes seeking to reproduce themselves you get crazy notions like this. They tell us that reproduction without the male of the species would be so much more efficient and helpful to the evolutionary process. Given, there are many predatory males that should NOT reproduce in this world, even if only fifty percent of their genes do get passed on, but to say we need to eliminate them all together is carrying it a bit too far. But again, evolutionary biology tells us that we need to find the "fittest" or most efficient way to reproduce in order to survive in this evolutionary world.

Regardless of your views on the theory of evolution, you have got to see the problems here. Why do we have sex? Why do we have movies? Why do we have baseball and football games? Why do we have music and the arts? Do they do anything to make our evolution more "efficient?" Entertainment, sports, music, and art have nothing to do with biology, but they all have to do with something we call "being created in God's image." It is what sets us apart from animals, trees, and amoebas.

A Nobel Prize-winning neurosurgeon once told his audience, on receiving his Nobel Prize, "I can explain how when you touch something it sends electrical impulses through your neuro-system and into your brain where it is interpreted through certain pathways and neurons. I can explain how light entering your ocular nerves can be converted into electrical impulses and sent to your brain for interpretation based on a database stored there. But I cannot explain with all my scientific knowledge why seeing my wife after a long day and touching my lips to hers causes and increases something in my life called joy and love. That is not the purview of science but the gift of a loving God."

Your Secret Identity

Who am I? Who are you for that matter? It is interesting to me to look into the ways that we describe and identify ourselves. For example: I am...

- a farm boy from Indiana
- a geek with glasses
- a jock taken out by knee injuries
- a singer
- an actor
- a college dropout
- a university graduate
- a master's graduate
- a husband
- a factory worker
- a factory supervisor
- a manager
- an upper level manager
- a business owner
- a father
- a father of teens
- a pastor
- a new church starter
- a speaker
- a professional speaker
- a fundraiser
- a writer
- a published author

- a mechanic (just changed my wife's brakes so feeling a little cocky on this one)
- a plumber (fixed the toilet this week)

Well, I think you get the idea. You could probably come up with a list of your own just as long or longer. But does this really describe me? Does this really tell you who I am?

Stop and think a minute. What phrase REALLY describes who you are? Not your occupation, not your position or status, and not even your dreams and visions. Who are you? When all else comes crumbling down, you lose your job, your dreams don't pan out, when your friends leave you…who are you?

Here's my answer; leave it or learn from it. "I am a child of God and I am loved." All else is window dressing. If all else falls away, this remains.

Who are you?

Smells

For those of you who don't know, my office is in a small shed in my backyard. I must walk off our back patio down a three-foot-wide sidewalk with the pool on my left and lawn on my right. Yesterday my son mowed the lawn and today as I write this I have my shed door and windows open. The smell of freshly-cut grass comes in with every slight breeze. I love that smell.

That smell conjures up pictures in my mind of summer days when school was out. It reminds me of rolling around in the grass as a kid playing games of adventure and heroism. It reminds me of laying on my back staring up at clouds as an amateur Rorschach test, comparing with my brothers and sisters. It reminds me of baseball fields that I played in and those my dad took me to in Chicago. I think it ultimately reminds me of home.

What a powerful thing smell is. I can sit here in my office and be transported back in time and space to anywhere, because of the smell of cut grass.

Every Sunday morning my dad drove all eight of his kids to church. During the service I would be seated on the left-hand side of him and my dad would cross his huge right hand across his chest and place his left elbow on it as an arm rest, while using his huge left hand to rub his weather-worn, freshly shaved chin and cheek. As I would lay against my father's side, fighting sleep and the urge to poke my nearest sibling, I would often slide my small hand into my dad's huge right hand, propping up his left arm. After a few minutes of this, Dad would move or I would and our hands would become disconnected. What does this have to do with anything? Well, my hand would smell like my dad's after this brief time. I would smell the slightly-faded aftershave still on his hand that had been transferred to mine. I still remember that smell and its connection to my father. While I don't remember a single sermon the minister gave, I remember the smell of love and responsibility on my dad's hands.

What a powerful thing smell is. Certain smells trigger memories of past girlfriends, past food experiments, and past mistakes. Smells trigger memories of places and times, both good and bad. Science will tell you that it is simply a combination of sensors and neurons that, in the right combinations, trigger this pleasurable response. I'll tell you that, while a grilled steak does make me salivate, the memories of grilling in the backyard with family and friends go beyond that pleasurable response; it's a God thing.

Elvis

This past week I went to one of the famous Las Vegas celebrity imperson-ation shows. It was quite an experience. I had never been to one before but, someone else paid so I kind of had to go. During that one-hour show I heard the voices of Joe Cocker, Bobby Vinton, Tony Orlando, Willie Nelson, Tom Jones, and, of course, Elvis. Now, Las Vegas is famous for its Elvis impersonators. This one had the hair, the outfit, the sideburns, and even the voice down. I never saw Elvis in person, only on TV, so I can't judge how good of a job this impersonator REALLY did, but I can tell you this: after about ten minutes of this Elvis, I was bored, I mean yawning bored, so bored I looked for a spot to take a quick nap. Half the show was dedicated to Elvis and thirty minutes was WAY too much time.

Now don't get me wrong. I like Elvis's music, especially "Suspicious Minds," but come on. Thirty minutes of a guy impersonating Elvis? If it had been the real thing up there, now that would have been something. Even die-hard Elvis fans can't listen to an impersonator that long. How many times can you hear the guy say, "Thank ya, thank ya very much," curl his lip, gyrate his hips, and wipe his brow with a scarf? That gets old pretty fast. I think even the impersonator was tired of the imperson-ation and tried to improvise for a little variety, but it just wasn't Elvis.

Who are you impersonating? Who are you "acting" like? All of us have heroes and favorites that we want to "BE!" Who is your choice? I see many young girls wanting to BE Brittney Spears. I see many young boys wanting to BE Kobe or the latest rap artist. I see many young men wanting to be like some successful mentor or person they've read about with the cars, jobs, and women around. Who do you want to BE? Elvis was never high on my list, but he must have been for hundreds of guys here in Vegas.

It is okay to emulate or impersonate another, especially if that person is a positive role model—someone like a parent, a big brother or sister, a teacher, or policeperson can be great people to impersonate. It can be like someone handing you a road map to a place they've gone and you haven't. Impersonating them can help you avoid pitfalls, U-turns, ditches, pot-holes, and everything else that can get you off track. But what happens when the person you imitate isn't so good? That kind of impersonation can lead you right into all those areas you want to, and should, avoid.

Take a look at your heroes. Take a look at those you would like to imitate. Cultivate, work hard at the ones that will be a positive influence on your life and starve out, through neglect, the bad ones. That'll keep you from being a hound dog and cryin' all the time; thank ya, thank ya very much.

New Discoveries

This week's news had two major new discoveries. First, the discovery of a new skull in Africa, which will "change the way we thought about the evolution of man." Then there is the gradual reshaping of our thoughts on dinosaurs. *US News* had its cover story on the NEW dinosaurs, the ones bigger than tyrannosaurus rex, and stranger than triceratops. Even the thought that birds are modern descendants of certain dinosaurs is falling by the wayside. Everything is new and changing. You might even say that our thinking is evolving. I also just finished the latest book by Stephen Hawking called *The Theory of Everything*, wherein he tries to reconcile Newtonian physics with quantum mechanics and observable evidence. He doesn't quite get there, but remains convinced that they would merge at one point.

What are we to think about all these changing discoveries? Textbooks on science, which were modern today, are out of date tomorrow. Firm, supportable theories yesterday are the strange ideas of today. The fact is, if Darwin were alive today, he would recognize very little of his theories of evolution still around. He believed in a static (unchanging) universe; we now know it is ever-expanding. He believed in a gradual, even evolution of species supported by the fossil record. Today's secular theories prove a "big bang" and a universe that moves in fits and starts, nothing gradual about it. Even Einstein battled against quantum mechanics because he believed there was no randomness in the universe.

Here's my thought—we will FOREVER be in a constant state of discovery, and that is GOOD. We will never be able to understand this universe and its complexity, yet we must try, because it is on the journey of discovery that we find out the important things. We cannot fear discovery and new ideas; we must savor them like a meal, roll them around on our tongues for a while, taste them, test them, and then either spit them out or swallow them—but never fear them.

I believe this world was created for our enjoyment, and part of that is the enjoyment of discovery and figuring things out. We find out about our lives, purposes, pasts, and places in this world when we dig into them. Plus, I believe this is a small taste of heaven. Heaven will be a constant and continual time of discovery, a slap on the forehead saying, "Oh, I get it now!" So dig in, because, as one of my favorite authors put it, "Science leads people away from God, GOOD SCIENCE brings them back."

Who is This Person?

Did you ever stop and look into the mirror and look; I mean REALLY look? Don't look at the imperfections in your skin or the makeup, or hair in place or not. Don't look at whether you need to shave or pluck or get rid of wrinkles. Just look at the person. I find myself wondering, "Who is that person?"

For my book cover I am having a "realistic" caricature done of myself. The artist doing it is extremely talented and I have seen his work where he can capture the look of a person in only a few lines on a canvas. I have had to pose for him a few times and then I had to give him some pictures of myself. He has shown me what he is working on and the samples. "Who is that person? Is that me? Am I really that bald? Do my eyes really slant that way? Who is that guy?" I think to myself. When others look at it, they remark at the likeness. Who is that guy? This artist is supposed to be good, but who is that guy?

Do you ever listen to yourself on video or cassette tape and wonder if that is REALLY what you sound like? Well I have that same feeling when I look at this painting of me. Is that really what others see that I look like?

Stop and think about the face we put on for other people. Think of the "masks" we wear to impress and hide. Really, what good do they do? I mean, people see us totally differently than we want to be seen anyway, so why confuse the issue even more with masks and many faces. Just be yourself. I mean, if they are going to see you the way THEY see you anyway and not the way you want them to see you, then what good is a mask? Shakespeare said in Hamlet, "God has given you one face and you have crafted for yourself, another!" You don't want to be known as two-faced in your life. So be comfortable with the person you are. It doesn't take long for the good people to see past the makeup and missing hair to the real person inside. The bad people? Don't worry about them.

As the artist develops my painting, I see lines disappearing and I see the character coming out—the "perceived" me. The one the others see, hmm, maybe this guy isn't so bad-looking after all.

The Contemplation of Air

It has been cooling off here in Vegas of late and I have taken the occasion to cut down on my electrical bill by turning off the air conditioning. I came home one afternoon to an empty house and an inviting couch. 92 degrees is mild for Vegas, but I thought it best to get a fan instead of turning on the AC. Turning the fan on low, I nestled into the couch for a quick "power nap." I developed the ability to power nap on the farm during the busy planting or harvest season. My brothers and I would be up early and into the fields, then called in to one of my mom's great dinners. (In Indiana dinner is the noon meal and supper is the evening meal, in between you would have "coffee time" at about 9:00 A.M. and "tea time" at about 3:00 P.M. We lived our lives around these social times on the farm.) After dinner we would lay down on the living room floor and within seconds fall fast asleep. We had no pillow and no couch, because we were dirty; just the carpeted floor on which to rest our weary bodies. Sometimes three or four brothers lay out on the floor. The crinkle of Dad's morning paper or latest farm magazine as he folded it back together brought us all to life and we piled back into the pickup and headed back to the fields.

While power napping I noticed the air blowing around me from the fan. With my eyes closed it felt as if waves of soft, cool satin were being wiped over me. Yet when I opened my eyes, there was nothing there but the feeling; nothing that I could see, and I could only hear the motor of the fan, not the air itself. I looked at the small hairs on my arms as they moved to the breeze and my thoughts turned to God.

There are a lot of analogies to God and his spirit in air. You cannot see them, you cannot hear them, yet you know they are there by the influence on all around them. Trees sway, hairs move, boats glide, and nations are changed, all by an unseen force.

Let me focus on another analogy that came to mind as I contemplated air on that Vegas afternoon. I looked at the fan. Now it is true that the air is still there and moving regardless of the fan, but the fan did something to it. The fan took the air, pointed it in a particular direction, and used it for the benefit of others—specifically, me. Now if you follow the analogy of air being God or his spirit, what is it that will point the spirit in a particular direction for the benefit of others? What came to my mind was prayer. Prayer takes the power and love of God and, at your request, points it at another.

So before I drifted off on my power nap, I turned on a few fans, pointed them at a few friends in need, then fell, smiling and cool, to sleep.

Traffic Birds

It did it to me again! I can't believe it! Just as I was getting up into the turning lane, the arrow turned yellow and quickly, too quickly, turned red as I pressed on the breaks to slow down. I know it saw me coming and with a smirk on its face tempted me with green, only to go yellow as I got close. You know who I am talking about don't you? That little smiling camera perched on top the traffic signals like a sparrow.

In Las Vegas we have our traffic controlled by a computer system with a series of cameras that can "see" the traffic and "judge" when and how fast the lights can change. Hundreds, if not thousands, of cameras perched on top the traffic lights keep silent watch over us early worms. There was not another car in sight, yet this all-knowing traffic computer decided to stop me at an intersection and make me wait. First the crossing turning lanes, then the crossing lanes got green (no one was there either), then just as I was ready to turn, the NON-turn lanes go and finally I get a three-second green arrow, a two-second yellow, and red again. I floor the gas pedal and screech around the corner just as it turns red. I could hear the traffic bird laughing—sending an email to his buddy at the next intersection.

Sometimes I just get the feeling that the person behind that computer or that program had an evil streak in them and liked to toy with vehicles at early morning hours.

One of the first computer games that came with windows that I got into was the card game "hearts." I was available on most Windows operating systems. I loved to play hearts as a kid and was pretty good at it. My brothers might beg to differ, but the computer game was fun. Once I mastered how the computer played, I could beat it pretty regularly, until I tried to "shoot the moon," which means that I tried to get ALL the hearts as opposed to the normal way of avoiding hearts. The computer cheated. There is no other way to say it. The computer cheated. EVERY time that I tried, the computer held its high hearts, even though I KNOW it wouldn't have known I was shooting the moon if it didn't cheat. It cheated! I can just see the programmer sitting at his desk at Microsoft, sipping his 15th cup of latte-mocha-macho from Starbucks at three in the morning, thinking: "What can I do to frustrate the experienced hearts player? I know, I'll cheat and have the computer look at his cards to see if he is shooting the moon or not. Yessssss…that's the ticket."

Okay, so maybe there isn't a malevolent presence in the program or in a traffic computer but, is there one in life? We believe all things work together for good, but do they always? I believe that the creator of this unbelievably intricate system we call life, had a purpose in you and I. And that gives me hope in a world that is seemingly chaotic. That gives hope when loved ones go off the deep end into self destruction or plain selfishness, the hope that in the end, GOOD will prevail. That gives hope when everything in your life seems to be falling apart into Humpty-Dumpty pieces. Knowing that good will win gives hope. Now, if I could just figure out how to time my commute to miss those birds.

Kleenex

Since moving out to Las Vegas I have been hit with allergies. Maybe "hit" isn't the right word; how about LAMBASTED with allergies? I don't remember a time since moving out here when my sinuses have NOT been full. I don't remember a time that I haven't been fighting headaches and a runny nose.

I have gone to the allergy doctor and he checked me out by shoving a "scope" of some kind up my nose. Then he took (what looked like) an air compressor hose and put an attachment on it that looked like a weapon straight out of the movie *Men in Black* and stuck that up my nose. I remember him saying, "This may feel a little weird," as he pulled the trigger. He was right; it felt weird for the next few days. He gave me expensive prescriptions and sample sprays to try. I did. At the end of it all I found that nothing helped more than ibuprofen for the headaches and Vicks nasal spray for the clogged sinuses, both of which can be bought at any drugstore for a few dollars a month rather than the hundreds of dollars for the doctors and the prescriptions.

One of my best friends during my walks with allergies has become my Kleenex box. I have one at my desk right in front of me. I have one in my truck. I also have one at the La-Z-Boy where I watch the news and read my papers. When I was on the farm as a teenager I thought Kleenex was for wimps. All you needed to do was lean over and do the famous "farmer's blow" and clean everything out quickly and efficiently, then wipe what remained on your shirtsleeve. I have noticed though, especially since I got married, that this time-tested technique isn't the most accepted way to clear your nose. I have had to adjust my methods a bit.

Who invented Kleenex? Somebody was walking around with a runny nose and his wife didn't want him to "blow" in the house so she handed him a sheet of sandpaper to blow in. He took the paper, and after blowing said, "Boy somebody should invent something that is a lot less harsh on your nose to blow into." Kleenex was born. Actually, according the to the official Kleenex website, Kleenex was invented in the 1920s to take off facial cream. Then in the 1930s it was marketed as a disposable handkerchief.

So where am I going with this? What is the spiritual application? I really don't know, but I thank God every day for the creativity he put in us to invent something like Kleenex—and so does my wife since she was grossed out by the "farmer's blow."

Family

I had the opportunity to walk along the a west coast beach in California recently and dream up ideas for this book, ponder the meaning of life, and to generally wonder how I am going to get the sand out of my shoes.

I would go out early in the morning and sit on some bleachers watching the teenage surfers as they floated on the water. I say floated because there weren't many waves coming in. Every now and again six or seven of them would catch a wave, four of them would immediately fall off, and then the next two while one would ride it into shore. There were a couple of the guys sitting next to me watching and commenting in some kind of "surfer dude speak" about the waves and the wipeouts. I didn't understand most of what they were saying even though it was English (I think), so I asked them: "How do you decide who gets the wave and who bails out?" They looked at me like I was from Mars and replied, "Just know man." "I'm sorry?" I replied. "Look man, if you got the wave you got the wave everybody just knows and bails." Interesting. I asked them if the containers ships docked off shore waiting to be unloaded hurt the waves. Out of their mouths came a combination of "dude, bogus, shifter, downer" and many other unrecognizable words, all of them pointing to "Yes, the waves are low because of the ships and they weren't happy about it."

I talked on the phone in the same week with my brother, the farmer in Indiana. Among other things he told me that he could not get some of his equipment repaired because the parts were hung up on the docks on the west coast or in those same container ships.

Think about that a minute. A dockworker strike on the west coast affected the surfer dudes in Huntington Beach and a farmer in Indiana, probably along with people in every state. We are ALL interconnected. What happens to one of us affects all of us in some way. This is one of those other things that make us human, different, and, as the Bible calls it, "Created in God's image." We are connected.

Do you remember the early waterbeds? You would push down on one end and the wave would pass through the bed and throw off the person in the other side of the bed. That is the wave that goes repeatedly throughout our nation and world when something happens. We are all, ultimately, family.

Epilogue

If you would like to receive Steve's weekly email of "Minding your Spiritual Business" send him an email at lvwunder@lvcm.com and you will be added to the list.

0-595-26336-4

www.ingramcontent.com/pod-product-compliance
Lightning Source LLC
Chambersburg PA
CBHW030800180526
45163CB00003B/1103